D1409899

DISTORTED TRUTH

DISTORTED TRUTH

What Every Christian Needs to Know About the Battle for the Mind

RICHARD J. MOUW

1817

HARPER & ROW, PUBLISHERS, SAN FRANCISCO

New York, Grand Rapids, Philadelphia, St. Louis
London, Singapore, Sydney, Tokyo

To the memory of
Larry Den Besten

FIRST EDITION

Library of Congress Cataloging-in-Publication Data

Mouw, Richard J.
    Distorted truth : what every Christian needs to know about the battle for the mind / Richard J. Mouw. –1st ed.
        p.   cm.
    ISBN 0-06-066031-7 : 14.95
    1. Apologetics–20th century.   2. Mouw, Richard J.   I. Title.
BT1102.M72   1989   89-45182
239–dc20   CIP

89 90 91 92 93 RRD 10 9 8 7 6 5 4 3 2 1

Contents

Acknowledgments

A few years ago, Larry Den Besten, then the Provost at Fuller Seminary, urged me to write a book based on my course, "Christian Worldview and Contemporary Challenges." I cannot now show him the finished product, but my dedicatory page is an expression of my deep sense of gratitude for the memory of his encouragement and friendship.

A word of thanks must also go out to others who have been important to the project: to Lew Smedes and Lois Curley for much good counsel along the way; to Tracy Scott for invaluable assistance and advice; to C. Davis Weyerhaeuser and the Stewardship Foundation for encouragement and support; to Dave Sielaff and Dirk Mouw for initiating me into the world of word processing; and to Phyllis Mouw for all that she has taught me about the search for an undistorted truthfulness.

1. The Hopes and Fears of All the Years

One winter afternoon in a Michigan shopping mall I received a theological suggestion from Perry Como.

At the peak of the Christmas shopping rush, I was making my way through the aisles at Sears in the hope that some gift idea would catch my eye. Instead, a phrase from a carol caught my ear.

I was vaguely aware of Perry Como's voice crooning songs of the season from the overhead speakers. But suddenly a line from "O Little Town of Bethlehem" invaded my consciousness: "The hopes and fears of all the years are met in thee tonight."

These words probably would not have attracted my attention if I hadn't already been puzzling about another line that I'd heard several weeks before, one from G. K. Chesterton. A speaker had quoted Chesterton as saying that the man who knocks at the door of the brothel is looking for God.

This had caught me up short. Isn't it obvious that the man who is ready to patronize a house of prostitution is hardly looking for God? Don't his actions demonstrate that he really doesn't care about God at all? Perhaps he's actually running away from God?

Though puzzled about the Chesterton quotation, I knew enough about Chesterton—solid defender of the Catholic faith that he was—to realize that he was neither stupid nor tolerant of loose sexual morals. He obviously was not meaning to say anything about the literal expectations people take with them to the doors of brothels—as if Chesterton thought that the man expected God to answer his knock!

Chesterton, I realized, was making an observation about the man's underlying quest. But how could the same point be made in such a way that it did not mislead?

That was what had been puzzling me for several weeks before Perry Como's singing caught my attention with the line about Bethlehem. I suddenly sensed that his words—actually the words of the writer Phillips Brooks—gave me a handle on my puzzle. Chesterton was encouraging Christians to probe beneath the surface motivations that brought the man to the door of the brothel. Look for the very basic "hopes and fears" that drive people to such places. That was his point.

And that was also the message of the carol: we must see the birth of Jesus as God's response to very real and very basic hopes and fears that people have.

I imagined the hopes and fears that surrounded me in the shopping mall. I began with surface sorts of things—that woman's hope that her husband won't come home drunk again from the Christmas Eve office party; that young man's fear that his fiancée will think that a red, lace-trimmed shortie nightgown is a stupid gift; the nine year old's hope for a new bicycle; the fashion model's fear of putting on too many pounds from all those holiday snacks.

The birth of the Christ child does not literally "meet" each of these needs one for one. But the salvation that Jesus brings does speak to the underlying issues—the hopes and fears, properly understood.

Thinking about these issues brought to mind the famous prayer of Saint Augustine: "Our hearts are restless until they rest in Thee." That is what both Chesterton and Perry Como were addressing: human restlessness. People are searching for fulfillment. And Jesus comes to "meet" the hopes and fears that drive us on in our restlessness.

Restless People and Their Ideas

This is a book about hopes and fears. I won't talk a lot about specific hopes and fears, but I'll have them in mind as I discuss the ways some major trends in our culture—some of the big ideas, the "isms" around which many people organize their lives—are shaped by human hopes and fears.

In this process we'll look at the connections between the restlessness that motivates people and the ideas they accept as true.

The Christmas season episode in that Michigan shopping mall almost two decades ago occurred early on in my career as a teacher of philosophy. The thoughts triggered by that incident have had a considerable influence on my work in the intervening years.

My early training in philosophy had placed great emphasis on analyzing arguments. In graduate school we did not pay much attention to human restlessness. Instead, we would study a passage in, say, Aristotle's writings, with an interest in whether Aristotle's arguments were good ones. We looked at how he presented his case for this or that conclusion, but we were not inclined to talk about his underlying hopes and fears. We did not ask why Aristotle was restless about the topic he was discussing.

I learned much from that approach. But I later realized I had also missed some important matters. When we were considering Aristotle's arguments of about the nature of change in the universe, we never thought to ask why it was that Aristotle was so interested in the topic of change. What fascinated him so about this topic? What were the hopes and fears that prompted his intense contemplation of the nature of change?

I still find it interesting to recall that Perry Como's recorded singing of the familiar carol amid the Christmastime rush in the aisles of a Sear's store nudged me toward focusing on that vital underlying dimension of philosophical exploration. Now in my philosophical thinking about contemporary issues and about trends evident in the daily papers, in newsmagazines, and in popular television commentaries ("Phil Donahue," "Sixty Minutes," and the like) I continue to focus on human restlessness.

The Peace Child

As it turns out, in my efforts to be a Christian philosopher who pays attention to the hopes and fears underlying this restlessness, I am learning from people in the Christian missionary enterprise who are exegeting (that is, digging out the meaning of) the culture.

Don Richardson records the discovery of a significant analogy to communicate the gospel in a tribal culture in *Peace Child* (my favorite missionary book).[1] This is a gripping account of the Richardson family's efforts among the Sawi people of Netherlands New Guinea. The Sawi legends celebrated treachery. Their heroes were men who betrayed those whom they pretended to befriend. The Sawi talked about fattening intended victims with friendship the way you would fatten a pig with food in preparation for slaughter.

Because of this long history of celebrating treachery, the Sawi people responded to the gospel story in a strange manner: they liked Judas. They considered him—the betrayer of Jesus—to be the hero of the story the Richardsons told them.

This initial evangelistic encounter left the Richardsons in shock. How do you communicate the gospel to people who come to the Bible with that sort of value system? Confused and disillusioned, they asked God for guidance.

The guidance was finally given a while later when they became aware of a practice whereby the Sawi people exchanged children with a hostile tribe. Each tribe would choose a healthy male child and give him to the other tribe. The little boy was called the peace child. As long as each of these boys lived, the respective tribes would not attack each other. But, of course, in this environment the life of a little child was not very secure. Children could easily die from a disease or an accident. So the peace that the exchange of these children brought was a rather unstable one.

This long-standing custom of exchanging peace children provided the missionaries with the opening they needed. Suddenly Isaiah's words came alive for them as a means of explaining the good news of the gracious redemption God has provided: "For to us a child is born, to us a son is given . . . and his name will be called . . . 'Prince of Peace.' Of the increase of his government and of peace there will be no end" (Isa. 9:6-7).

The peace child ceremony gave the Richardsons a glimpse into the restlessness that was at work beneath the surface of the Sawi value system. They were able to see something of the basic hopes and fears that shaped the lives and beliefs of the Sawi people. And they were able then to speak about the ways in which those hopes and fears were "met" in the birth of Bethlehem's Child.

What the Richardsons went through is a good example of a process that another missionary writer, Kosuke Koyama, describes in his book *Water-Buffalo Theology*.[2] He says that if we are going to communicate the Gospel effectively to our non-Christian neighbors we must exegete (dig out the meaning of) two different things. We must exegete the Bible, but we must also exegete the culture to which we are sent.

Good missionaries, says Koyama, will always find themselves "sandwiched between" these two realities: the reality of God's word and the reality of the cultural context they are trying to address. That's what the Richardsons were doing when they found a match-up between a biblical theme and a Sawi ceremony: exegeting both Bible and culture. And that's not an assignment just for missionaries who journey to far away places.

Hopes and Fears

North American Christians have often been more sensitive to people's hopes and fears when proclaiming the gospel to other cultures than they have been on their own home soil. This has been true of the kind of Christianity with which I identify most closely. Evangelical Christians have been very concerned about truth. If somebody denies the doctrine of the virgin birth of Jesus, we are quick to point out that they are accepting false teachings.

This is not to say that there is anything wrong with having a deep commitment to truthful thinking—I have no desire to defend heretics.

But it is also important to probe beneath the surface of error to see why people are attracted to false systems of thought. It is one thing to say true things, such as "Jesus was born of a virgin." It is another thing to understand why people are not inclined to accept those truths. The Richardsons could have stood in the center of the village announcing that Jesus is greater than Judas until they were blue in the face, but it was much more effective to probe for the hopes and fears of a people who seemed to be so obsessed with treachery.

I'm not saying that we should never denounce falsehood. The Nazi regime was founded on lies, and Dietrich Bonhoeffer lost his life because he was willing to stand up for the truth. I am not suggesting that he should have engaged Hitler in dialogue, probing beneath the surface of his error to try to understand the hopes and fears that made nazism such an attractive way to look at life.

That would not have been helpful. Hitler's thugs were slaughtering millions of people in the name of their system of thought. This was no time for patient listening or leisurely philosophical discussion. The Nazis were evil people, and they had to be told so in no uncertain terms.

But neither does that mean that it is silly to ask probing questions about nazism. Stopping Hitler did not put an end to the kind of *thinking* that shaped his wicked deeds. There are still people around who are drawn to "master race" ideologies. If we are going to eliminate these ideas we must get around to asking those probing questions. What are the hopes and fears that make these systems of thought so attractive to people? Why do some of our human neighbors accept such wicked schemes?

Being Fair to "Isms"

In this book I will try to ask probing questions about some of the big ideas that are influencing people in our culture today. I have chosen some formative patterns of thinking and acting, each of them an "ism" that has gained the loyalty of people whom I know in North America: humanism, monism, occultism, nihilism, relativism.

All these "isms" have at least one thing in common: they have all been severely denounced by some Christians, especially Christians from that part of the church I know best. And in each case I agree with the basic stance these Christians are adopting. All these "isms" are untruths. They are fundamentally misguided ways of looking at things. When I meet people who have accepted one or more of these "isms" I want very much to tell them that they are on the wrong track.

But I am also not happy with the way these "isms" are treated by the Christians who take such a strongly negative stance. I have already observed that these are the people who are inclined to assess non-Christian thought with a rather single-minded focus on truth. Paradoxically, though, this fixation on the truth often leads to many untruths. By issuing a dogmatic pronouncement about a specific "ism" Christian people regularly miss much of what is going on in the pattern of thought and action that the "ism" represents.

I once heard a Christian leader give a speech in which he denounced homosexuality. He gave the impression that people choose to be homosexuals and that therefore the only reason why anyone might experience homosexual inclinations is because of his or her own willful desire to be a wicked person.

I was able to get a few minutes alone with this leader to tell him how upset I was about his distorted account of the nature of homosexuality. I told him about a student of mine who pleads with God every day to change him into a heterosexual, with very little success thus far. This young man doesn't know of any choice that he ever made to be the way he is. He is an evangelical Christian who devotes much energy to attempting to lead others to Christ. But he struggles on a daily basis with homosexual fantasies and desires.

As I related my concern to this Christian leader a sneer formed on his face. Finally he broke in: "You intellectual types always want to complicate things for the rest of us with your fine points of argumentation. But I want nothing to do with your qualifications and compromises. What this country needs is a return to the old-fashioned morality of the Ten Commandments. That's what I preach, and I will continue to do so, no matter what people like you say!" He turned and walked away.

Unfortunately this Christian leader doesn't seem to want to pay attention to the fact that "the old-fashioned morality of the Ten Commandments" includes God's own insistence that we not bear false witness against our neighbors. Truthfulness is very dear to the heart of the God of the Scriptures. We do not serve God well when we misrepresent the people whom we are criticizing.

This concern for truthfulness should also motivate us to be fair about the non-Christian "isms" that are influencing so many people today. We cannot settle for cheap victories over unbelief. Honesty and fairness cannot be sacrificed as we engage in spiritual warfare. We must make a sincere attempt to understand the very real restlessness that leads people to commit their hearts and minds to the intellectual spirits of the present age. We must be willing to engage in self-criticism even as we offer our assessments of other systems of belief.

"Communion Rail" Faith

Recently I reread George Reedy's fine little book *The Twilight of the Presidency.* Reedy was a special assistant to President Lyndon Johnson, and his experience in the White House led him to be critical of the way the office of the presidency is currently structured.

At the end of his book Reedy explains why he is so willing to be critical of accepted political practices. Some of his friends might even be a little surprised, he observes, to find him being so critical. They know him to be, he says, "a very devout man. I accept literally the concept of the virgin birth, the trinity, and the resurrection." But, Reedy continues, "the basic point is that my unquestioning faith begins and ends at the communion rail. On all other matters, I reserve the right of skeptical judgment. And I believe that the only real blasphemy—the deadliest of sins— is the deification of mortals and the sanctification of human institutions."[3]

Reedy has a good sense of the proper spirit of critical questioning. And he is also right about where that spirit is best cultivated.

It begins and ends, he says, "at the communion rail." Critical questioning, if it is going to be healthy and consistent, will flow from the heart of a person who worships the true God.

This means, for one thing, that we Christians are not talking about an "ideology" that we cling to for dear life. Our ultimate commitment is not to a set of principles but to a Person. It is not that ideas and principles are unimportant. They are very important. But they are not what is *ultimately* important to us. At the center of things is a God who calls us to worshipful obedience.

It also means that the kind of critical questioning we engage in cannot be of the arrogant, smart-alecky sort. When we have worshiped in the way the Bible prescribes, we will experience humility and awe and a sense of mystery. These are hardly the ingredients that go into the making of an arrogant spirit.

We do need, then, a place at the center of our lives where we experience an unquestioning faith. This is a requirement that many non-Christians will find difficult to understand. They will insist that a genuinely open mind must be open to everything, even to criticisms of the basics of the Christian faith.

But this is misleading. People who talk this way are really putting their own personal critical faculties at the center of things. They are insisting that God and everything else must satisfy the demands of their own questioning spirit. From a Christian point of view, this does not really seem very open-minded at all. The Christian believer wants to insist that genuine open-mindedness is found in the attitude expressed by the psalmist: "Search me, O God, and know my heart! Try me and know my thoughts!" (Ps. 139:23). Authentic open-mindedness means placing our whole being before God's gaze for his critical scrutiny. This is the kind of open-mindedness that leads us, as Reedy puts it, to "the communion rail."

The assurance that I worship a wise and powerful God, then, is a basic "given" for me as a Christian. And because of this conviction, I do not have to be afraid to ask some fundamental questions—even questions about how I can best formulate my understanding of what God's wisdom and power are all about.

To ask such questions can be a very helpful way of making sure that I am putting my trust in the right place and not just relying on my own fabrications.

The Apostle Paul draws the boundaries for us very nicely. In his first epistle to Timothy, he warns us against false teachers who enjoy asking questions and playing around with words — these are the marks of a corrupt mind that has no interest in the truth (1 Tim. 6:3–5). But in his second epistle to Timothy he clarifies his meaning. He tells the church to avoid the kind of argumentation that is "stupid" and "senseless" (2 Tim. 2:23).

That is important advice. Critical questioning can indeed be done in the wrong spirit, with a desire merely to confuse and complicate things. But it can also be aimed at clarifying our thinking, at helping us to focus on God's wisdom and authority rather than our own inclinations. This latter kind of critical questioning is just the opposite of "stupid" and "senseless" argumentation; it is wise and learned.

This is a book for people who have gained enough confidence "at the communion rail" to try to ask some wise and learned questions about the "isms" they see around them.

2. How to Fight for the Truth

The minister at Faith Bible Church likes to be called Pastor Tom. It took a while for the parishioners to get used to that form of address; they would never have thought to call Tom's predecessor by his first name.

And that wasn't the only change that Pastor Tom brought with him when he arrived at Faith Bible Church eight years ago. As the church members put it to each other when they talk over coffee, the preaching in their services has become "much more relevant to our everyday lives." Pastor Tom is one of a new breed of fundamentalist preachers. Fundamentalists are "Bible-believing Christians" who have placed a strong emphasis on "separation from the world." Tom himself was trained in that kind of perspective—in which the church is viewed as a place where people get ready for heaven.

But Tom now thinks that the church should also prepare Christians for active lives in *this* world. Like other fundamentalist preachers who have identified with the religious New Right, he has begun preaching about what is going on in the everyday world. And his church members, many of whom are community volunteers and lawyers and managers, are enthusiastic about his ministry.

Tom feels that he is at his best when he is speaking about those issues of contemporary life that have a very obvious "spiritual" connection. Even though his parishioners know where he stands on the evils of abortion and pornography and on the need for a strong national defense, he really doesn't think of himself as preaching about a lot of "political specifics." His task as a minister of the gospel, as he sees it, is to make people aware of the spiritual forces that are at work in contemporary life.

The world is, on Tom's way of viewing things, a spiritual battle-ground. In one sense, there are many forces contending against each other on this cosmic battlefield. These are the various "isms" around which people organize their lives. But on a deeper level there are really only two parties to the conflict: God and Satan.

When Pastor Tom instructs his church members how they are to understand what is going on in the world he urges them to keep these two basic parties to the cosmic conflict clearly in mind. As they think about feminism and abortion on demand and the teaching of evolution in the schools and the proper stance for America to adopt in dealing with the Russians, Pastor Tom wants them to ask; Who is on the Lord's side, and who is promoting the cause of the Evil One?

And it isn't just a hit-and-miss matter as we approach the important struggles in our world with these concerns in our minds. There are rather clear ways of deciding whether something is of God or of Satan, Pastor Tom insists. Both God and Satan have what Tom likes to call "philosophies of life." God's philosophy is spelled out clearly in the Bible. In simple terms, it is a view of life in which God is at the center of things; people have been created to honor and serve the Lord of Life. Satan doesn't like this philosophy. He wants human beings to see themselves as being in charge of the basic patterns of their lives.

When Tom wants to know what is the right side and what is the wrong side of some matter important to society, then, he uses these two philosophies as his reference points. How do the issues look if we put God at the center of things? And how do they stack up when we think of human beings as being in charge of the show?

For Tom the basic pattern is spelled out clearly in the third chapter of Genesis. There the two philosophies of life are laid side by side. God has told Adam and Eve that they are not to eat the fruit from the tree that stands in the middle of the garden. But the serpent challenges that divine restriction. He tells Eve to go ahead and eat from the tree. When you do so, he promises her, "you will be like God" (Gen. 3:5).

Tom is quite fond of the Genesis 3 account. He refers to it very often in his preaching. He wants his people to be clear about the need to take sides in the cosmic conflict.

Taking Responsibility for Culture

I find much to celebrate in the way Pastor Tom conducts his ministry. This is not to say that I agree with everything that he and his like-minded colleagues are trying to accomplish. On the contrary, I would want to lodge my strong protest against many of their analyses and proposals. But we mustn't allow the angry attacks on "the New Right preachers" in recent years to obscure the fact that the Pastor Toms of conservative Protestantism represent an important—and in many ways an exciting—religious development.

Pastor Tom rightly senses that there is something seriously wrong with two characteristics that have dominated his part of the Christian community for many decades: otherworldliness and anti-intellectualism. Tom represents a generation of fundamentalist leaders who have been trying to correct these traits.

Otherworldliness comes in different varieties. Some otherworldly Christians have operated with a strong conviction that physical reality—the world of sights and smells and sounds—is vastly inferior to the spiritual realm. These people have argued that Christians must detach themselves as much as possible from an affection for physical things.

The fundamentalists have worked with a somewhat different emphasis. Even though they have often expressed much enthusiasm for "spiritual blessings," their antipathy towards "the things of this world" has had less to do with a denigration of physical reality as such than with a rather pessimistic reading of the historical process. They have insisted that as the world moves toward "the last days" human society will become more openly sinful. Indeed, the process of cultural degeneration will finally go so far that only a miraculous divine intervention, in the form of the return of Christ, will alter the flow of things.

Before we can argue intelligently with a group of otherworldly Christians we need to understand the *basis* for their otherworldliness. If it has to do with a conviction that the physical realm is vastly inferior to the world of the spirit, then we can try to get them to develop a more positive view of the relationship between the two kinds of reality. But if their perspective stems from a pessimistic reading of cultural development, then our task is to convince them that they need a more hopeful outlook on the historical process.

That is basically what has happened to the Pastor Toms. They have become more hopeful about what is happening in the contemporary world. The reasons for this shift are complicated, and it is not necessary to go into them here. Suffice it to say that many fundamentalist Christians have begun to feel that they still have a genuine opportunity to influence the course of events in the larger society. Whereas in the past fundamentalists typically resigned themselves to feeling that nothing could be done to clean up the mess in the world, now many of them are sensing an obligation to work for social improvement.

This change of cultural perspective has also had implications for the anti-intellectualism that has been such an obvious presence among the fundamentalists in the past. I don't mean to say that fundamentalist Christians ever opposed the intellect as such in any consistent sort of way. One of the better-known "Bible institutes" once had as its promotional slogan "Our only textbook the Bible." Strictly speaking, of course, this was false advertising. Students at that school were assigned readings from many books *about* the Bible, as well as writings that dealt with doctrinal and historical topics. In fact, that particular Bible institute was associated with a publishing venture that was a major supplier of biblical commentary to the conservative Protestant community.

Of course, no one can really be against *everything* associated with the intellect. We have to think about how much garlic should go into the spaghetti sauce and whether we can make it through another year without buying a new car.

The kinds of Christians who have spoken disparagingly about

"the intellect" really have "worldly learning" in mind. They have worried about becoming tainted by what they view as the corrupt philosophical systems of this sinful world. Rather than taking any chances, they have simply withdrawn from the scholarly-intellectual discussions of the larger human community.

Intellectual Warfare

The fundamentalists have often been the most zealous proponents of this kind of anti-intellectualism. Scholarly pursuits can only complicate the issues, they have insisted—better to nurture a simple faith that "just takes the Bible at its word."

In recent decades, though, many fundamentalists have started to show a serious interest in scholarly discussion. An interesting illustration of this change of attitude is a 1980 book, *The Battle for the Mind*, by the fundamentalist leader Tim La Haye.[1] La Haye's critics have often been so disturbed by some of the brash claims that he made in his book—he insisted, for example, that the major institutions of American life (political, educational, journalistic, entertainment) were under the control of a network of 275,000 humanists—that they have failed to take note of the significant shift of mood that La Haye was signaling. His title itself conveyed an important message: the fundamentalist troops were now being rallied for a campaign on an *intellectual* battlefield.

Tim La Haye wanted fundamentalists to see the error of thinking that their "simple faith" was sufficient for the struggle against "worldly learning." He wanted them to combat the unregenerate mind with a *regenerate* mind. Satan has a carefully devised intellectual strategy for opposing the truth of God, La Haye insisted. If we Christians are to counter this strategy in an effective manner, then we must have a carefully devised intellectual strategy of our own.

And it is obvious that Tim La Haye is no lonely prophetic voice in the fundamentalist world. Many conservative Protestants who were once given to downplaying the importance of education have become strong supporters of Christian schools. And although it is legitimate to be a bit cynical about Christians who suddenly became interested in private education right around the time that racial integration became mandatory for the public school system, it would be wrong to dismiss their concern as nothing more than racism. Such a motive would not explain, for example, the way fundamentalists, who were once quite satisfied with "Bible institutes," have begun to build Christian liberal arts colleges and theological seminaries.

Fundamentalists, Pentecostalists, and other Christians who have long nurtured anti-intellectual patterns have recently gained enthusiasm for the *intellectual* battle against unbelief. And that is an important discovery.

My willingness to see this as a positive development will bother some people. Fundamentalists make them nervous, and they are not inclined to feel less nervous when the fundamentalists begin taking education seriously. Look at the strong "military" tone the fundamentalists use as they arm themselves for the intellectual battle, these critics would say. The old warfare against moral evil has now branched out into a "battle for the mind." Isn't it unhealthy to inject a spirit of militancy into the intellectual enterprise?

Understanding the Battle

There is one good thing that can be said about warfare imagery: the Bible uses it quite often. And it is difficult for Christians to ignore this portrayal. There *is* a struggle going on in the universe, and our intellectual lives figure into that struggle. The Apostle Paul makes this very clear: "We destroy arguments and every proud obstacle to the knowledge of God, and take every thought captive to obey Christ" (1 Cor. 10:5). The fundamentalists are on solid biblical ground when they insist on the reality of a *battle* for the mind.

The question is not *whether* we are called to engage in intellectual warfare. It is how we are to *conduct* ourselves in the battle. And this is where many zealous Christians often show great insensitivity. They do not act like proper Christian warriors.

How are we to behave in the battle for truth? Well, for a start, truth is a good thing to think about. Our Christian battle for the mind is meant to serve the cause of truth. We must fight the battle as honest people who are trying to be truthful about ourselves and others.

This means, for one thing, making sure we have correctly identified the contending parties. If there is a battle going on, who are the parties to the struggle?

Fundamentalists claim to be fond of simplicity. They like to tell us that "the issues are clear." They take great pride in their ability to draw clear lines between righteousness and unrighteousness, truth and error.

It is tempting to criticize these patterns by arguing that things are not always so simple. But in this case the fundamentalists have not been simple enough. They have obscured the battle lines by not focusing on the *really* fundamental issues.

In the simplest biblical terms the real battle that is going on in the universe is between God and Satan. These two are the only "absolute" antagonists. This means that we should not be too quick to see an argument between two *human* groups in cosmic terms.

The danger of identifying the cosmic battle too closely with the differences between human antagonists is nicely illustrated in the first chapter of Jonah. The prophet is on a ship heading for Tarshish. The ship's crew are pagan sailors who rely on superstitious practices when they come upon stormy seas. Jonah, by contrast, is a servant of the Lord who is not afraid to bear witness to his faith when disaster threatens: "I am a Hebrew; and I fear the Lord, the God of heaven, who made the sea and the dry land" (Jon. 1:9).

We seem to have a clear example here of truth against error, biblical orthodoxy versus pagan superstition. But not so—the sailors rightly identify Jonah as the cause of their problems, and they chide him for his disobedience to his own convictions. Here is a story in which unbelievers play an important corrective role. I once heard a fine sermon on this text in which the preacher put the point this way: we have a case here where the world preaches a much-needed sermon to the church.

Abraham Kuyper, a nineteenth-century Dutch statesman, emphasized what he called "the radical antithesis" between belief and unbelief.[2] He was calling attention to the very deep differences between Christian and non-Christian ways of seeing things. But Kuyper was often surprised when he worked with unbelievers in public life. The unbelieving world, he said, sometimes acted better than he expected it to, while the church often acted worse than he would have predicted. This shows, he argued, that the basic conflict is not so much between *people* as it is between *principles*. People aren't always consistent with their principles.

The only two actors in the cosmic drama whose performances we can count on are God and Satan. God is consistently truthful. Satan is always bent upon deception.

Once we get to the level of human performance, though, the lines are more difficult to draw. Pogo's proclamation has a good biblical ring to it: "We have met the enemy and they are us!" Even at our best we Christians are often wrong. And we are seldom at our best. Unbelievers, on the other hand, are often correct in what they think—sometimes unwittingly, but also at times wittingly.

This is not to deny the fact of a cosmic struggle between truth and error. But it is to insist that we will often misidentify truths and errors if we think in rigid "us versus them" categories. The cosmic struggle reaches into our own hearts. Each of us is a battleground where skirmishes occur on a regular basis. This warfare will not end until that day—which is surely coming for every redeemed child of God—when we will finally be made perfect. Until then we would do well to exercise caution in how we draw the battle lines.

Choosing the Right Armor

It is also good to be clear about how best to equip ourselves for the battle. An obvious biblical reference point here is the "whole armor of God" passage in Ephesians 6. Actually, this passage has often been used to foster the kind of arrogant spirit that many people identify with the fundamentalist mentality.

It isn't difficult to see how the arrogance gets started. We read what the Bible says about spiritual warfare, and we come away with at least these two convictions: we are called to fight, and God provides us with armor to protect us in the battle.

And both these convictions are legitimate. The arrogance gets planted in us, though, only if we lose sight of some other details about the warfare to which we are called.

One detail has to do with the item just discussed: the identity of the enemy. The enemy is not merely "out there" but is also to be found on our own internal battlefield. Once we see this, then the armor of God described in Ephesians 6 becomes necessary not just as protection from the threats that external forces pose to us, but also as a defense against those dangers that arise from within our own hearts.

Another crucial detail deals with the manner of our warfare. How are we to fight? What weapons and tactics will we employ? What spirit do we bring to the conflict? Here too arrogance seems out of place in people who are equipped with the armor of God as described in Ephesians 6. Think of the moral and spiritual attributes associated with these pieces of armor: the girdle of *truth*, the breastplate of *righteousness*, feet that are dressed in the gospel of *peace*, the shield of *faith*, the helmet of *salvation*, the *word of God* as our sword.

Commodities like truth and righteousness and peace are often in short supply among militant Christian crusaders. Nor do we always see that kind of faith that is so clearly displayed in Psalm 139, in which the poet who vows that he hates the Lord's enemies with a perfect hatred also sees the need for an assault on the enemy that lurks within his own soul: "Search me, O God, and know my thoughts! And see if there be any wicked way in me" (Ps. 139:23–24).

The failure to use the Christian "sword"–the word of God– properly is a crucial factor in Christian arrogance. We touched on this in the previous chapter. Militant Christians often act as if the divine command not to bear false witness against our neighbors doesn't apply when our neighbor is a homosexual or a feminist. New Testament teachings about the importance of compassion and love are regularly ignored. Christians tend to wield the sword of the Spirit in a very selective manner.

The Renewal of the Mind

Many Christian pacifists shun warfare language completely. They recognize that the Bible uses battle imagery, but they are convinced that these images have been so misused by Christians that it is better to avoid them.

I appreciate these concerns, but I still use warfare imagery. My understanding of the Bible's battle language is that God is reminding us that a conflict is being waged between good and evil, righteousness and unrighteousness, truth and falsehood. Though I recognize the dangers of a militaristic spirit, I also think we need to take the reality of a cosmic struggle very seriously.

An old Quaker image provides us with an alternative to the usual pacifist rejection of warfare images. The early Quakers described their pacifist way of life as "fighting the Lamb's war." They insisted that Jesus calls us to a new *kind* of warfare, in which a meek and gentle spirit is the primary weapon.

Even though I'm not a pacifist, I like that approach to the Bible's warfare language. All Christians, whatever their specific views about the permissibility of violence, should operate with a transformed understanding of what warfare is all about.

And we must extend this to intellectual warfare. Think of some of the things that the Apostle Paul identifies as "works of the flesh," things like "enmity, strife, jealousy, anger, selfishness, dissension, party spirit" (Gal. 5:20). These are the sorts of things that often characterize intellectual conflict.

Think too of some of the things Paul lists as "fruits of the spirit": "patience, kindness, goodness, faithfulness, gentleness, self-control" (Gal. 5:22–23). To display these positive characteristics as we go about our intellectual tasks is to transform our ways of thinking. And that is just what we are encouraged to do in the twelfth chapter of Romans: "Do not be conformed to this world, but be transformed by the *renewal of your mind*, that you may prove what is the will of God, what is good and acceptable and perfect" (Rom. 12:2, italics added).

In the New Testament, "proving" is an intellectual activity that is closely related to "discerning" and "testing the spirits." A necessary element of caution and modesty is built into these activities. The person who understands the need to "prove" and "discern" and "test" is not someone who will leap to quick conclusions or always opt for the tidy answers. Indeed, to avoid the "quick fix" kind of thinking, and to refuse to settle for slogans, clichés, and proof texts, we have to struggle against certain tendencies in ourselves as we engage in Christian intellectual warfare. The Christian "battle for the mind" includes fighting off the temptations of shoddy thinking and cheap rhetorical "victories."

Mars Hill Militancy

I once heard a Bible teacher argue that the Apostle Paul's speech to the folks on Mars Hill was a big mistake. Since this teacher also subscribed to a very strong view of the Bible's "inerrancy," he was quick to explain that he didn't mean that Luke's account of that speech in Acts 17 was faulty in any way. On the contrary, he said, what we find there is an inerrant report of a bad sermon! On this teacher's view, the Holy Spirit inspired Luke to include Paul's speech in the Book of Acts so that we would have a reliable account of how *not* to go about evangelizing pagan philosophers.

I have a much more favorable impression of the apostle's sermon. But the Bible teacher's response was instructive. He rightly sensed that Paul's methodology on that occasion does not sit right with the militant spirit many conservative Christians have when they approach "pagan philosophers."

Again, I am not questioning the importance of being militant for the truth. But it is important to let the Bible tell us *how* to be militant. And the Mars Hill encounter seems to be a passage given to us for that kind of instruction.

Let us assume, then, that the apostle was being appropriately militant in his approach to the Athenians in Acts 17. What can we learn from his example about the kind of militancy God wants to see in us?

One thing we can learn is that militancy does mean having strong convictions about the gospel. There was nothing compromising about the spirit that Paul brought to this encounter. The story begins with the observation that as the apostle observed the religious situation in Athens, "his spirit was provoked within him as he saw that the city was full of idols" (v. 16).

Paul recognized that he was dealing with an idolatrous culture, and he knew that idolatry was directly opposed to true religion. Nor did he hide these convictions in his address to the Athenians. The true God, he tells them in unmistakably clear terms, does not dwell in the shrines that we humans fashion. Everything else receives its reality from him (vv. 24–25). This God will be satisfied with nothing less than our repentance.

Paul's militancy also illustrates the importance of affirming our common humanity. The apostle goes out of his way to emphasize the underlying bond of humanness that links him to his audience. All of us have received our "life and breath and everything" from God (v. 25). All the peoples of the earth, Paul proclaims, are created "from one" (v. 26). Together we are all "God's offspring" (v. 29).

Conveying a sincere respect for our opponents as human beings might well have a good effect on them, making them more open to what we have to say. But that isn't the only reason for cultivating this attitude of respect. It is also important to recognize what the attitude can do for *us*.

In his discussion of the work of civil authorities in his *Institutes of the Christian Religion,* John Calvin offers some rather specific advice to rulers who find it necessary to take up arms against an enemy. Calvin is no pacifist, and on a quick reading of his comments he seems merely to be rehashing the main points of what has come to be thought of as "just war doctrine." But a careful examination of Calvin's advice reveals some very interesting points. He warns the rulers to be careful not to be influenced "even in the slightest degree" by such passions as anger, hatred and "implacable severity." And then he expresses the hope that those in authority will "have pity on the common nature in the one whose special fault they are punishing."[3]

This shows a profoundly biblical insight into the way our sinfulness functions in situations of human conflict. Typically, when nations go to war they put the best possible interpretation on their own motives and the worst possible on their enemy's. Calvin is insisting that we reverse this pattern. He knows we are very quick to overlook our own faults and to magnify the faults of others, so he recommends a corrective exercise: before you attack someone take a very honest look at your own sinful passions, and cultivate a good sense of the humanity of your enemy.

This exercise applies as well to our intellectual warfare. To repeat a point I made earlier: often the intellectual battle is as much against our own sinful tendencies as it is against the errors of others. And since we are generally inclined to be easy on ourselves and rough on the views of other people, it is a good thing to follow Paul's example when he emphasizes the human bond that links him to the Athenians.

Another item illustrated in Paul's encounter is the necessity of recognizing that our opponents are participants with us in an important spiritual quest. God placed all human beings on the face of the earth, Paul tells his Mars Hill audience, so that "they should seek God, in the hope that they might feel after him and find him" (v. 27).

This description does not apply only to people who are already Christians. It is obvious that Paul has in mind people who have not yet found the true God but who can be properly thought of as "feeling after" him.

In one sense, of course, it is obvious that these Athenians are on some sort of spiritual quest. They have built all sorts of shrines, and they have even inscribed one of them with the words "To an unknown God" (v. 23).

But this isn't how Paul knows that their searchings are spiritual in nature. He hasn't simply inferred this from the fact that they are altar builders. He knows that they are spiritual seekers because he understands God's creating purposes. We have been *fashioned*, Paul insists, in such a manner that we long for the God who made us.

Remember Chesterton's brothel customer. How does Chesterton know that this man is on a spiritual quest? Knocking on a brothel door is not immediately identifiable as a "spiritual" activity! But Chesterton knows something about the purpose of the God who fashioned the man. He knows that this person has been created with spiritual longings, with a deeply rooted need to satisfy the ineradicable hungers of the soul.

Chesterton's example makes it clear that what we see as a spiritual quest will not always be described that way by the people we are observing. But that isn't the deciding factor. We are assessing their words and deeds in the light of what we know about the creator's purposes.

Finally, Paul's approach illustrates the importance of attempting to put the basic concerns of our opponents in a favorable light. There are two ways of interpreting this requirement, and each is legitimate. One is as a gesture of courtesy. By formulating our opponents' positions in the most favorable way we can increase the likelihood that they will take our own perspectives seriously.

Much attention has been give in recent years to the patterns of successful communication. Many of us have read books and articles, or attended workshops or seminars, that are devoted to heightening our "listening skills" and our ability to "share" in effective ways.

These are good things to be concerned about, and they have an obvious relevance to intellectual dialogue. It is often extremely helpful to tell our conversation partners what we think we have heard them saying, or what we are able to affirm in their stated positions, before going on to explore serious differences. Beginning an important discussion with an attempt to find points of agreement or areas of common concern can be a way of putting our opponents at ease, so that they will be more open to what we have to say.

This is to concentrate on the need for intellectual courtesy. And again, that is no insignificant matter. Many of us in the Christian community have much to learn about this kind of etiquette.

But we must also pay attention to the second way of interpreting this requirement, in which the emphasis is on gaining understanding rather than showing courtesy. Putting the basic concerns of our intellectual opponents in a favorable light doesn't only help them to be more open to us but also can help *us* to understand the issues more clearly.

This brings us back to "the hopes and fears of all the years." It is seldom enough simply to declare someone's position to be erroneous. That may be all that we can do in a crisis—Nazi Germany was the example we used earlier—but such declarations do little to promote understanding between our opponents and ourselves.

But why worry about promoting mutual understanding with unbelievers? This isn't just a silly or mean-spirited question. Good Christian people raise it, for example, when they hear about proposals for inter-religious dialogue. These proposals trouble them. How can a true Christian have genuine "dialogue" with a Buddhist? Doesn't a willingness to enter into dialogue mean that we are open to having our minds changed? And isn't that precisely what we are not open to when we talk with Buddhists? Aren't we Christians convinced that Jesus alone is the savior of humankind? How can we engage in "dialogue" about that nonnegotiable conviction?

Again, these concerns must not be dismissed as either silly or mean-spirited. If we believe, as I do, that people can be saved only by accepting Christ as savior and lord, then the idea of dialogue about basic convictions is a troublesome one.

But I do think the notion of dialogue can still be rescued. To engage in dialogue does mean an openness to possible changes in the way we view things. It is to look for a new understanding of the issues. The important question, though, is of *what* issues?

Here is what I *cannot* say as I enter into dialogue with non-Christians: "I believe that Jesus is the only true savior of humankind, but this is not to say that my mind cannot be changed. Let's talk together about it, shall we?"

But here is what I *can* say: "I believe that Jesus is the only true savior of humankind, and it is difficult for me to understand how people who deny his lordship can find satisfying answers to the basic issues of life. I'd like to understand better how people like you wrestle with the fundamental issues. Let's talk about it, shall we?"

Christians ought to be eager to enter into the kind of dialogue that helps us better understand what makes other people "tick." We ought to want to eliminate misunderstandings, to clear away intellectual and spiritual obstacles to a more effective communication of the gospel.

Here again the missionary example seems appropriate. The Richardsons were changed by their encounter with the "peace child" people. As they exegeted the Sawi culture they had to set aside their initial misconceptions. Ultimately they gained a much richer understanding of the meaning and power of the gospel. Yet at no point did they sacrifice their basic conviction that the Sawi people desperately needed to accept Jesus as their divine deliverer.

Mars Hill Methodology

The encounter at Mars Hill in Acts 17 has been much discussed by scholars as a case in point for questions about how much people can find out about God apart from the Bible. And it is not difficult to see why it is considered to be an important apostolic encounter. Paul seems to credit his audience with quite a bit of spiritual sensitivity. He even uses lines from some of their own poets in proclaiming the reality of the living God.

Is Paul positing a "common ground" between believers and

unbelievers? Is he attributing to pagan religion a limited but laudable kind of knowledge of God? Those are some of the questions that have been debated. But we do not have to settle them here. For our purposes a few modest comments about Paul's treatment of the Mars Hill perspective will be enough to set the tone for our discussion of our own intellectual encounters with our non-Christian contemporaries.

The apostle studied the Athenian perspective on reality. He entered into a very real dialogue with the Mars Hill crowd. Dialogue includes two stages: listening and responding. When the Apostle Paul spoke to the Athenians he made it clear that he had been "listening" to them. He had observed their shrines, studied their inscriptions, and read their poets. When he addressed them he was in effect responding to what he had seen and heard.

He probed for evidence of a spiritual quest. He approached his encounter with them with the conviction that these people were created for fellowship with the living God. Their statues and shrines and poetry and philosophical speculation were all seen by Paul against the background of a deep spiritual hunger.

He looked for positive points of contact in their experience. He probed for themes in their thinking that he could build upon in talking about the gospel with them.

Whether this means that the apostle posited some sort of religious "common ground" between himself and the Athenians is, of course, a matter for debate.

Suppose I say to a Ku Klux Klansman, "You seem to be yearning for a strong sense of communal identity. You want to be able to say that you really *belong* to something. And that is a *good* thing to want."

In talking this way have I established "common ground" with the Klansman? Perhaps it could be construed that way—although that makes me nervous, given my revulsion against the Klan's view of reality. But I certainly have found a legitimate point of contact with the Klan member. And in my remark to the Klansman I have looked for some deep concern that informs his quest for belonging. In singling out the search for a sense of identity I am probing a need to which the gospel speaks in a very direct manner: Jesus died on the cross so that we sinners can be given a new identity as the redeemed sons and daughters of God.

This is the kind of thing that Paul was doing on Mars Hill. He affirmed the spiritual impulses that motivated them to build their altar "to an unknown God" (vv. 22–23). And against their observable tendency to reduce the divine to something they can manage (vv. 24–25), he quotes "even some of your poets" in support of a much grander view of God's being and power (vv. 28–29).

He invited them to turn to Christ in true repentance. There is no mistaking the evangelistic impulse at work in Paul's approach to these people. And that is always a laudable impulse. We ought to want people to turn to Christ—even if we can't always issue the invitation with the apostolic boldness Paul displayed when he was giving an invited speech on Mars Hill!

But this does not mean that all of Paul's preparation for the evangelistic appeal was a mere tactical ploy. In this encounter the apostle genuinely engages those to whom he speaks. He probes in an intelligent way the agenda of their hopes and fears. And I am inclined to think that this probing is in itself a good thing— even if the evangelistic appeal produces no harvest of souls.

When we allow ourselves to be taught by the apostolic example we gain a new understanding of what militancy for the truth is all about. We see the need for an empathetic probing of "the hopes and fears of all the years." As we speak to others about the claims of the gospel we must allow their spiritual quests to enlarge our own hearts and minds. Doing so can help us testify more effectively to the power of God.

But it isn't just that we listen so that we can be better communicators of what we already understand; the dialogue is also necessary for our own growth in understanding.

When I finished reading Don Richardson's *Peace Child* for the first time I was thrilled at the way the Sawi people had come to understand that Jesus is the Prince of Peace. But it wasn't simply that *they* had come to grasp the gospel; in the process of learning about this encounter I had gained a greater sense of what that gospel is all about.

The same kind of thing should happen to us in intellectual dialogue. Those encounters help us grow in our knowledge of the truth.

When we seriously engage the thoughts of other people—even people with whom our disagreements run very deep—we have an opportunity to learn some new things about "the hopes and fears of all the years." And the desire to gain that sort of understanding is a very important feature of a properly fought battle for the mind!

3. Giving the Devil His Due

It was a surprisingly awkward conversation, and I was disappointed. I had been looking forward to meeting this person.

He was a tenured professor at his university, an accomplished scholar. He had been a Christian now for about a year. Not long after his conversion he had happened upon an article of mine and written to me about it. We had corresponded back and forth a few times. When I realized I was to be traveling to his university town, we had arranged to meet. But now that we were actually talking together he seemed very ill at ease.

Finally he admitted it. "Look, I'm really nervous. This may seem strange to you, but you're the first Christian academic I've ever talked with about my faith. I've got all kinds of questions I've wanted to ask, but right now they all seem so elementary I'm embarrassed to ask them. I've spent all these years in academia, and all of a sudden it's as though I'm thinking about intellectual issues for the first time!"

That broke the ice, and soon the conversation was everything I had hoped it would be. He should not have felt intimidated. His "elementary" questions were really very profound probings.

One of his topics of concern was the Devil. "Before I became a Christian I thought a belief in Satan was a leftover from the Dark Ages—something you found today only on the lunatic fringe. But now as I look back on my own pre-Christian days, I sense that I was held in the grip of a power that tried to dominate my thoughts. Becoming a Christian meant being released from that stranglehold. In Christ I am now free to see things in a different way."

The look on his face was pleading —the kind that says, "Tell me you don't think I'm crazy!" And that is exactly what I did tell him.

The Devil's Reality

The history of thinking about the Devil has been chronicled in great detail by Jeffrey Burton Russell. He has written four much-acclaimed scholarly studies on the subject, tracing the theme from ancient times through the New Testament and the early church, through Jewish, Christian, and Muslim thought in the Middle Ages, and through the Reformation to contemporary times.

Professor Russell's books have focused on how the idea of the Devil has functioned in religious thought. But in the final pages of his fourth book he reflects in more personal terms on the plausibility of this idea as an item of religious faith. He expands further on that subject in a review article in *Commonweal* magazine:

The Devil has become embarrassing to many modern theologians caught up in secularist patterns of thought, but any nonbeliever or clear-thinking believer will want to consult two millenia of Christian tradition including the New Testament with more interest than the latest critical and theological theories of contemporary academics. Like it or not, belief in the conflict between Christ and Satan is an integral part of Christianity that can be removed only by ruthlessly tearing apart the fabric. If some modern academics are correct, and Christianity has been dead wrong on a central issue from its very inception, why bother with Christianity at all? One must take Christianity or leave it, and not shoehorn it into the latest theories from Paris or the Black Forest.[1]

The recent convert to whom I spoke had "taken" Christianity, and he was now experiencing the tension Professor Russell describes. Secularism tells us that belief in the Devil is a relic from the past. Yet many of us see it as an important element in the Christian way of viewing things.

I believe in a personal Devil. For one thing, I share Russell's assessment that Satan's reality is "integral" to what is taught in both the Bible and the theological tradition.

But I also have an experiential basis for my belief in the Devil. I frequently consider doing bad things—and only slightly less frequently I actually do bad things. Another way of putting this is that I regularly experience, and succumb to, temptation. And when I am struggling with temptation I have a strong sense that I am being tempted *by* someone.

Now, I don't intend to be pulling off some sort of "proof" here for the Devil's existence. You can believe that people are tempted by a variety of things without being compelled logically to posit the existence of a Temptor.

But as I reflect upon my own experiences of temptation the idea of a Temptor seems to fit very well. I mean, of course, the serious temptations, not the ordinary tug of war with chocolate cake and procrastination and the fleeting desire for things I know are bad for me. I'm thinking of the big struggles—the meanness that I sometimes actually plan out, the lustful thoughts that I allow to linger in my mind, the feelings of revenge and envy that I nurture.

Sometime during the seventh or eighth century Saint Andrew of Crete wrote a hymn dealing with our Christian warfare against the forces of evil. Here are two of his verses:

> Christian, dost thou see them, On the holy ground,
> How the powers of darkness Compass thee around?
> Christian, up and smite them, Counting gain but loss;
> Smite them; Christ is with thee, Soldier of the cross.
>
> Christian dost thou feel them, How they work within,
> Striving, tempting, luring, Goading into sin?
> Christian, never tremble; Never be downcast;
> Gird thee for the battle, Watch and pray and fast.

I am personally familiar with the struggle Saint Andrew describes. The notion that there are spiritual beings that "work within" me—"striving, tempting, luring, goading into sin"—makes good sense to me.

When I succumb to wicked impulses I regularly feel that I have acceded to a power that *wanted* me to yield. And when I refuse to give in to evil, I regularly sense that I have thwarted a force that had designs for me.

In short: for me, being tempted is being goaded *by* someone. My soul has an enemy. This foe is a real center of consciousness who wills the worst for my life.

A standard criticism of this way of viewing the Devil's role in our lives is that it encourages us to evade responsibility. And no doubt people can misuse the notion of an Evil One in this way: "The Devil made me do it!"

I am not saying, though, that Satan "makes" me do anything. When I choose to do something that is bad, that really is *my* choice. But in making the choice I was responding to someone's goading. The lure of evil is not an accidental thing. It is a part of a organized campaign. There is a power in the universe that tries to enlist us in a program of opposing the good.

Our Rebellion

I also find the Devil to be philosophically interesting. There is an intellectual basis to Satan's organized opposition to God's purposes. The Devil's program can be seen as dealing with each of the three areas discussed by developmental psychologists: the affective, the volitional, and the cognitive. Satan is concerned with how we feel, how we will, and how we think.

This is clear in the approach taken by the snake of Genesis 3, identified in the Book of Revelation as "that ancient serpent, who is called the Devil and Satan, the deceiver of the whole world" (Rev. 12:9). He attacks Eve's feelings of trust toward God: Did God say *that*? Don't take it seriously! He just wants to keep you ignorant!

And Satan obviously wants our first parents to make a rebellious choice. He is eager to have them pit their will against the divine will.

But he also deals with their basic understanding of things. The serpent aims at a cognitive shift. He presents Adam and Eve with a set of philosophical alternatives. Either God is at the center of things or human beings are. Up to this point the first man and woman have accepted God's authority as supreme. In giving into the temptation to "be like God" (Gen. 3:5), they are shifting from a God-centered conception of reality to a human-centered one.

Doesn't this strong emphasis of mine on the Devil's "philosophy" make me sound quite a bit like Pastor Tom? Yes it does. As I view things, the fundamentalist "battle for the mind" people start in the right place. But I need to emphasize the fact that it is only a start.

I once worked on a committee that had to write up a theological statement that began with some comments about the nature of sin. The assignment of writing a first draft of the opening section fell to me. We were a fairly like-minded group, and I wrote out a few paragraphs that I thought would be quite acceptable to everyone.

I was surprised, then, when several committee members questioned the tone of my comments. They thought that I had put too much weight on the idea of sin as rebellion. Is it really helpful, they asked, to make that our central category for explaining the sinful condition? When we label people as rebels, aren't we treating them as hostile and obstinate in their attitude toward God? And, if so, isn't this an unfair and unhelpful way of approaching many flesh-and-blood unbelievers?

Their point was a helpful one. So I have to be careful here in the way I express my agreement with the Pastor Toms. I want to say that it is a good *start* to observe that a cognitive rebellion occurred in the Genesis 3 story.

Adam and Eve did rebel against God. And their disobedience is ours as well. "In Adam's fall / we sinned all." The rebellion of our first parents is the preface to the human drama that unfolds in the Scriptures and in our own lives. But my committee members were right to worry about an approach that addresses unbelievers as active rebels.

Consider an analogy. Rachel is a teenage runaway. At age three she was adopted by a couple who tried to give her love and affection. But Rachel seemed bent on rejecting their efforts. By the time she was thirteen she was experimenting with drugs and promiscuous sex. Now at age fifteen she is one of New York City's "street children."

Is Rachel a "rebel"against her adoptive parents? In one sense, yes. She is in her present situation because she resented their authority and spurned their love.

Suppose, though, that we attempt to reach Rachel with this message: "You are a rebel, living in open disobedience against your parents' authority. You must surrender. Repent and return home!"

This will not speak to her actual state of mind. Rachel is confused, lonely, hurting, abused. She feels unlovable. Nor is this all a smokescreen that she is using to hide her "real" feelings of rebellion. Rachel is genuinely immersed in the deepest kind of hurting and hopelessness.

This is how many people experience their separation from God. They are not inwardly shaking their fists at their creator; they are caught up in a profound mood of pain and despair.

An apparent biblical counterexample comes to mind. Didn't the prodigal son of Jesus' parable have to recognize his rebellion before he could be reconciled with his father?

We must be careful, of course, about trying to get too much theological meaning out of the specific details of the biblical parables. This story , for example, is not meant as a model for how to evangelize pig-feeders! Even if we focus on details, though, the parable doesn't really support a primary emphasis on rebellion. When the son "came to himself" his first observation was "I perish here with hunger!" (Luke 15:17). Only after he recognizes his desolate condition does he sense the need to confess that he has sinned against his father (v. 18).

Our sinful state has its origins in a rebellion against God. This rebellion has a cognitive dimension, and we all share in it— something deep within us makes us balk at the notion that God's authority is at the center of things. But our alternative perspectives on reality cause us real pain and loneliness. We can feel genuinely lost in the worlds we fashion out of our refusal to honor God, and it is often in that feeling of desolation that the gospel touches our lives with a promise of love.

How the Serpent Lies

It may seem as though I am trying to put two moods together that don't really fit each other very well. On the one hand, I am treating unbelief as a satanic way of viewing reality. On the other, I am trying to foster an openness to the very real "hopes and fears of all the years" that operate in the lives of unbelievers.

Don't I have to choose one way or the other? Aren't sinners either proponents of a satanic worldview or confused and hurting people—but not both?

This simple either-or choice is precisely what we must avoid. To give in to it is to fail to see how Satan himself operates. Pastor Tom and his colleagues get off to a good start, I have said, in their emphasis on the encounter with Satan in Genesis 3. As they proceed, though, they miss some important nuances.

Before looking at the nuances, let's review the points that they have understood correctly.

They are right to see that *the serpent is a liar.* Genesis 3 tells us about two differing perspectives on reality. One of them puts God at the center of things; the other organizes reality around human authority. Satan propounds the latter view. But it is a lie, and Satan knows it.

The serpentine lie is a very basic one. It is not just one of your everyday (in this case "garden-variety" would be a poor choice of words!) untruths; it is a lie that pierces to the very heart of things. Everything hangs on the issue at stake here. Either God is in charge or we are. The fundamental reference point for understanding reality is either God's way of viewing things or ours.

And *the serpent persuades Adam and Eve to accept the lie.* A basic cognitive shift actually occurs. Sin is, to be sure, more than a way of thinking; it is also a way of feeling and choosing. But the cognitive is one important aspect.

Now let's look at some nuances. I'll first state them briefly and then we can look at some of the issues in more detail.

The serpent is a subtle liar. Satan isn't stupid. His skill in tempting people was obviously recognized by Jesus himself. Jesus' encounter with the Temptor in the wilderness was something he took very seriously. Satan probed at issues that lay at the heart of Jesus' messianic mission. He is rightly thought of as the *Great* Deceiver. And his manipulative skills are already obvious in the Eden encounter.

The serpent's lie is a distorted truth. It is not just a straightforward falsehood. Satan doesn't just deny the truth, he twists it. The lie of Genesis 3 is an impressive one—it had to be, to bring about all that damage. This is a falsehood we must be sure to understand correctly.

The serpent probes at deep hopes and fears. He initiates his conversation with Eve by asking a question that zeros right in on fundamental issues of authority and self-image. He gets her to fear that God does not want what is best for her. And he holds out the hope that she can realize new potentials.

Satan's Subtleties

Lying is a complicated business. Sissela Bok makes this clear in her excellent book *Lying: Moral Choice in Public and Private Life.*[2] We tell "little" lies to patients who are dying and to children who can't handle adult answers to the questions they ask. We tell "big" lies to our nation's enemies and to people who have already lied to us. We tell white lies; we offer lame excuses; and we withhold the truth to protect confidentiality.

Some lies are blatant falsehoods. Other lies are not "simply" false. They twist the truth rather than straightforwardly denying it.

Satan is a twister of the truth. This fact about him is signaled in the opening line of the Genesis 3 story: "Now the serpent was more subtle than any other wild creature that the Lord God had made" (v. 1). We are given reason to expect some subtlety in the serpent's approach to humankind. And he doesn't disappoint us.

In the opening pages of his *Institutes* John Calvin observes that our knowledge of ourselves and our knowledge of God are intimately intertwined: if we don't understand ourselves properly we can't understand God either—and vice versa. The serpent grasps this point well. When he talks to Eve he hones right in on her understanding of herself and of God. When you eat the forbidden fruit "you will be like God," Satan tells her (v. 5).

"You will be like God." This is the serpent's lie—*the* lie—the untruth that is not simply a blatant falsehood but a distorted truth.

What exactly is the truth that the serpent distorts? It is the clear teaching of the first chapter of Genesis, that the man and the woman are fashioned in the very "image" of the God who created them (Gen. 1:26–27).

The meaning of "the image of God" has been much debated by theologians, and the arguments continue. We don't need to go into all the disputed points here. A few general observations will be enough for our purposes.

Human beings image God in a unique way. The whole creation bears the stamp of its Creator. Just by looking at our universe we can learn something about the divine splendor. "The heavens are telling the glory of God; and the firmament proclaims his handiwork" (Ps. 19:1). But human beings reveal something about God in a special way. When we look at men and women—especially when they are functioning in the ways the creator intended—we should be able to gain insight into God's character.

The image of God is complex. Theologians have proposed many different attributes for status as *the* one way in which we uniquely resemble God: the fact that we have a "spiritual" side to us; or that we can reason; or that we make free choices; or that we—like the members of the divine Trinity—are social beings; or that like God we are capable of exercising "dominion" (Gen.

1:28). It may be that one of these is more central than the others. But it is also likely that *all* of these things figure into our "imaging" of God.

There is a special dignity associated with the image. Dignity can be found throughout the creation; animals and plants deserve more respect than we have usually given them. But they are not the same as human beings. When the psalmist rehearses the creation story he celebrates the fact that we humans have been "crowned" with a unique kind of "glory and honor" (Ps. 8:5). Being created in the divine image means that God treats us in a special way: God recruits us for important tasks and takes delight in the gratitude and praise we are able freely to offer him.

The image of God theme is a splendid one, and Satan knows it. Rather than ignoring it or denying it outright, he twists it. "You will be like God," he says to our first parents.

The serpent is playing on a subtlety. He knows full well that the man and the woman are already like God. So, subtle beast that he is, he distorts this wonderful truth.

The Genesis 1 creation account gives us one sense of what it means to be "like God," the God-imager sense. That's the good way in which we imitate God. If I know that I am a God-imager, I understand something about who God is and who I am. I know that I am *not* God. I don't stand at the top of the ladder of being. I'm not the ultimate judge of what is good and true and healthy. I reflect something of God's glory, but I'm not its original source.

Satan introduces another sense of what it means to be "like God." This is the God-pretender sense—where "pretender" has the same meaning as in "pretender to the Spanish throne." In this sense human beings claim the right to stand in God's position of authority, to run the show themselves.

The serpent was taking advantage of God's handiwork. Adam and Eve could be tempted to become God-pretenders only because they were already God-imagers. The perverse desire to sit on the divine throne made sense to them only because they already basked in that throne's reflected glory.

The Trust Factor

We had been talking in class that day about the relationship between faith and reason. The sorts of things I had said seemed quite acceptable to most of the students. This was a Christian college, and I had not said anything to shock their evangelical sensitivities. Besides, most of them were taking Introduction to Philosophy only because it was a requirement for graduation.

Susan was an exception. She had a strong philosophical bent and was easily the brightest student in the class. On this occasion she was upset with me, and she stayed after class to tell me about it.

"You made it all sound so easy, but it isn't! 'Rational arguments can't demonstrate basic Christian beliefs – but that's OK, since we don't need them anyway.' How convenient! I'm getting tired of being told that it all hangs on faith!"

She paused for a moment. Then her tone became almost pleading. "I'm sorry to sound sarcastic, but I do have a hard time believing. In church yesterday morning the preacher made it sound like you are a horrible person if you have any doubts. Then we sang this simple-minded hymn about what a firm foundation we have in the Bible. One line in the hymn really grated on me: 'What more can He say than to you He has said?' Well, I'll tell you, I can ask for something more – a *lot* more. I'd like a real proof of God's existence. Or how about a video recording of Jesus coming out of the tomb?"

I couldn't bring myself to tell her that "How Firm a Foundation" is one of my favorite hymns. But we did have a good talk – and many more after that – about the nature of faith.

What about Susan's complaints? Were they legitimate? Well, yes and no. She was both right and wrong in her demand for "something more."

Susan was exploring the proper boundaries of religious trust. Christianity requires that we believe that there is a God, and that Jesus was raised from the dead (among other things, of course). But it takes quite a bit of trust to believe these things. And it's not just blind trust. We need something to work with in order to generate the requisite trust. But how much do we have a right to ask for?

Trust is a tricky phenomonen. There something about trust that smacks of paradox. And I'm not thinking here just of religious trust. Trust in general—including ordinary, everyday trusting—has a paradoxical feel to it. When I trust it is both legitimate and illegitimate to want more than I have to go on.

Let's split this paradoxical sounding claim into its component parts. When I trust someone it is legitimate to want more than I have to go on. A wife begins to worry that her husband has been unfaithful. When she tells him about her suspicions he responds with fairly convincing assurances of his fidelity—*fairly* convincing. She decides that she has to trust him. But it takes some effort. Sometimes,when she thinks about it, she wishes she could be sure.

That's the way it goes with trusting. If she were sure, then she wouldn't have to trust. Suppose someone told her that her husband was seen dancing cheek-to-cheek in a Chicago night club on Friday night. And suppose she knows that her husband was playing Scrabble with her in Wichita on that very evening. She wouldn't have to say, "But I trust my husband." She could just say, "I know that can't be true."

But it is not legitimate to expect trust and unimpeachable certainty to go together. If the wife wants to eliminate any room for doubt, then she should not expect the relationship to be held together by trust. This is not to knock unimpeachable certainty. There is much to be said for that cognitive commodity. But we must be clear that when we eliminate doubt we also eliminate the need for trust.

Is this just to fool around with words? Not at all. It is important to see that the thing we call trusting finds its place only in those relationships in which there is some room for doubt.

I must make it clear, though, that I'm not saying that we aren't really trusting people unless we are feeling doubt about them. In a telephone conversation with my son, I ask him how his studies are going. I trust the answers he gives me. That doesn't mean that I'm actually fighting off doubt when I accept his reports as true. But it does mean that doubts could be raised about what he tells me. You might ask me, "How can you be sure that he isn't making it all up? Maybe he dropped out of college a month ago and has been actively involved in art thefts. How can you be sure you're not in for a rude awakening one of these days very soon?" The answer is that such doubts have never entered my mind, but now that you bring them up, I have to say that though I can't be absolutely certain that your story is false, I really do trust my son.

To trust is to accept and believe when there is also room for doubt. When I trust, I reach for more than I am able to grab hold of.

Susan complained about not having enough to go on in her struggles with faith. One way to take this is as a complaint about the need for trust as such in religious matters. Why should such an important area of life have to be held up by trusting ? Why can't we just be certain about God and the resurrection and the afterlife?

Note that in this case Susan would not be asking that her religious *trust* be based on unimpeachable certainties. That would be to show confusion about what trust is. She is expressing the wish that religion not be held up by trust at all.

Susan has a right, of course, to prefer that religion be something very different than it is. But I am not at all convinced that we would be better off if the trust element were completely absent from our lives.

I would certainly not want trust to be eliminated from relationships in general. It might be nice if on this or that occasion we could be more certain about what is really going on in the hearts and lives of other persons. But it would also be unfortunate if *all* the guesswork were removed.

It is good for us to learn to trust—and to learn to be trust*worthy*. With trusting comes commitment and fidelity and other valuable things. I'm pretty sure that I would not want to be the kind of being for whom the question of trust never arose.

Trust and Humanness

But I want to make even a more basic point: trust is central to what it means to be a human being.

I'll go even further. If you were to ask me for my best shot at a one-line definition of humanness, I would give you something like this: the human person is a *trusting* being.

Offering capsule definitions of humanness has long been a pleasant philosophical pastime. Without question the most influential of these definitions is the one Aristotle offered. What makes us human, he says, is that we are "rational animals." Christian thinkers have often found this to be an attractive way of getting at the essence of humanness. But I don't think it does the job.

Consider the question of whether a computer could ever really "think." In recent years there has been quite a bit of interest in the "minds and machines" topic. I find those discussions intriguing.

Sometimes, though, both sides in the debate take it for granted that if we allow for the possibility that a computer might really think, then we have finally gotten rid of any notion of human uniqueness. This is a very Aristotelian conviction. If the only thing that might account for our uniqueness as humans is that we are rational, and if now the machines that we have invented can also exercise rationality, then we have invested our machines with the one thing we thought only a human being could possess.

Let me tell you what I would consider to be an amazing breakthrough in computer technology—not just a computer that could reason in the ways that human beings reason, but a computer to whom it would be necessary to issue the advice of Proverbs 3:5: "Trust in the Lord with all your heart, and do not rely on your own insight."

The basic contrast in this piece of biblical wisdom is important: we should trust in the Lord rather than rely on our own cognitive powers. In one obvious sense, of course, it is good to rely on our own insight. God gave us the ability to think, and he wants us to use it—but not in such a way that it takes the place of trusting in God. To "rely" on our own abilities in the bad sense is to look to our own cognitive abilities as the basic guide for living our lives. That's how the serpent wants us to "rely"—"You will be like God."

I personally have no doubt that some animals—apes, for example—engage in a kind of thinking, a rudimentary rational problem-solving. But I don't worry that an ape will put its basic trust in its own insights. And I don't worry about computers in that regard either. Only if an ape or a computer started to have that kind of problem would I begin to worry that they were becoming like us humans.

It is interesting too that the Proverbs verse mentions the "heart" as the part of us that does the trusting. That is a common biblical theme. "Heart" here is not simply the part of us that pumps the blood; it is our spiritual center.

Writers on spirituality these days often refer to "centering prayer." This kind of prayer does not concentrate on addressing God with petitions or ordered thoughts. It is more a releasing of oneself to God's presence. It is centering oneself on God.

This very intimate "space for God" is the same as the biblical "heart": my innermost self; the spiritual place where my basic allegiances are formed; the secret arena where my trustings get started.

It is in this intimate centering space that we are either for or against God. Either we are trusting God as we set the direction of our lives, or we are trusting something else.

From a Christian perspective, then, everyone's life is directed at the core by some kind of trust. It's not that some of us have "faith" and others build their lives on reason or science or "the flow." Rather, the question is *where* you are putting your basic trust: your own ability to think? collective human expertise? what feels right? the wisdom of God?

Please understand that we are talking about *basic* trust here, and about what in the most fundamental sense we are trusting *in*. To put my basic trust in God doesn't mean that I may not trust my wife or son, or that I should be skeptical about what careful thinking comes up with, or that I should give no weight to my hunches. It does mean, though, that I have to understand clearly that one trust relationship that undergirds all my other trustings.

Satan's Flexibility

The Devil doesn't want us to obey God. Outside of that, though, he's pretty open-minded. Anything goes. Satan is flexible. That's a crucial fact to keep in mind.

The sinful life comes with a lot of options built into it. Sin is giving our basic trust to something other than God. That leaves us with all of created reality to choose from.

It is important not to try to squeeze all sinners into the same mold. In his essay *Of True Religion,* Saint Augustine gives a quick inventory of sinful perspectives that he observes in his own culture. Sinful people love and worship God's works rather than God himself, and different people, Augustine says, choose different works as their favorites.[3]

Some people worship the human soul or the human body. Others worship animals or inanimate objects. Still others, Augustine observes, venerate the sun or the moon or the stars. And then there are those who "think themselves most religious" because they worship "the whole created universe"—"the whole of this together they think to be one great God, of whom all things are parts."

Some of these preferences are crude. Others seem rather sophisticated. But Augustine is right to insist that in the final analysis the differences do not really matter to God. What matters is whether our worship is directed toward the Creator or the creaturely.

Satan is anti-God. This means he is content with any choice that we make from among the many options available to us as we scan the creation for something to trust.

But we mustn't conclude that the Devil pays no attention to specifics. He works hard to match us up with the creaturely option that best fits our individual interests and needs. He pays careful attention to our actual hopes and fears.

And that's why it is also good for us to focus on hopes and fears if we want to begin to undo the great harm Satan has caused. Indeed, without attending to hopes and fears we will not adequately grasp the nature of the harm sin has brought into human life. Sin began in rebellion, and our first parents' rebellious manifesto—"We will be like God"—still echoes loudly around us.

But sin also brings other things into our lives; deep aches that won't go away; wounds that run so deep that we are convinced no healing balm could ever touch them; desperate loneliness; guilt; fear. None of this should surprise us. It isn't just that we have redirected our allegiance from the Creator to something creaturely. We have also cut ourselves off from the One who alone *deserves* to be trusted by the likes of us. And for beings who are especially designed for trust, that is very sad indeed. "Our hearts are restless until they rest in Thee."

We are going to look now at some of the actual "isms" that compete for our trust in contemporary culture. It is important to remember that these "isms" are some of the means people use to give shape to their restlessness. If we fail to interpret properly the actual hopes and fears that feed this restlessness, then we can easily miss some of Satan's subtleties.

4. Honoring Humanness

The letter began, "Dear Visiting Humanist." And even though I was a surrounded by strangers, my first impulse was to look over my shoulder to make sure that no one could see what I was reading.

This was my first day as a postdoctoral fellow at Princeton University. I was one of a group of eight people visiting the university that year under a program funded by the National Endowment for the Humanities. Standing in line at a campus coffee shop, I was going through the small packet of mail I had just picked up. This letter was about a reception on campus to which we visiting fellows were invited. Since we were all scholars who worked in the humanities, we were greeted as "visiting humanists."

My nervous reaction to that mode of address made me realize how skittish I was about that "humanist" label. Just a week before I had read about some Christian parents who were so upset about secular humanism in the public schools that they were scouring textbooks for evidence of anti-Christian influences. Someone had found a reference in a history book to the importance of "humanistic studies." In the context it was obviously an allusion to scholarship in the humanities. But this group of parents would have nothing to do with that kind of fine distinction. To them the reference was yet another example of the glorification of "godless humanism."

I took my coffee cup to a table and quickly entered the information about the reception into my pocket calendar. Then I tore up the letter and threw it away. I chuckled to myself. At least if I dropped dead in the next few minutes the evidence of my local reputation as a "visiting humanist" would not be found on my person!

The Uses of 'Humanism'

"Humanist" is a label that is put to many uses. I have just pointed to one of them—a "humanist" as a practitioner of the humanities, someone who teaches, say, literature or philosophy.

There is certainly no need for Christians to oppose this kind of humanism. To be sure, we might have strong ideas about how Christians ought to work with the subject matter of literature or philosophy. But that is different from opposing the humanities as such.

There is another sense of "humanism" that also seems quite compatible with a Christian commitment. Indeed many devout Christians have used the label in this sense to refer to some of their deepest convictions. Jacques Maritain, for example, one of the best-known Catholic philosophers in this century, was a strong defender of the Christian faith against secular alternatives. He liked to call himself a "Christian humanist." And an important study of John Calvin's social perspective bears the title *The Social Humanism of Calvin.*

When the term is applied to people like Maritain and Calvin it signals a belief in the fundamental worth of the human person. In their thinking about political and economic issues, for example, both Maritain and Calvin place a strong emphasis on policies and practices that respect the dignity of each individual.

You don't have to be a Christian to believe in human worth, but Christian humanism is one way of emphasizing that worth. And *Christian* humanists will have a different way of explaining why it is that human beings are so valuable. Christians believe that human worth is in a significant sense derived. We are valuable because God values us. We can't adequately understand our human worth without recognizing that we are created by the loving God who sent Jesus to redeem us.

At the university where I was a graduate student in philosophy, one campus group took the name "The Humanist Society." They had a hard time finding speakers for their meetings, so they asked me to give a speech responding to their strongly anti-

Christian brand of humanism. I explained the views I have just attributed to Maritain and Calvin, then I invited them to think seriously about exchanging their present brand of humanism for this variety.

That was back in the days before my fellow conservative Christians had launched a full-scale attack on "humanism." I could still afford to be a little playful with the label. And I would gladly own the humanist label yet today if given adequate time to explain myself.

But that sort of luxury does not come easily anymore. The net result of the recent Christian crusade against humanism has been our relinquishment of the term to unbelievers. If Calvin and Maritain were alive today they would be well advised to look for another label.

In giving up the label, though, we have run the risk of obscuring an important issue. By attacking everything that goes by the name humanism we could easily mislead people into thinking that we Christians are opposed to any viewpoint that places a high value on humanness. It would be sad if that were the impression we gave. From a Christian point of view, the question cannot be *whether* to value humanness but *how* to do so.

What is the nature of that humanism that Christians have been attacking so vociferously in recent years? It is the teaching that human beings are the ultimate authorities regarding the basic issues of life.

Note the difference between this emphasis and the conviction of the Christian humanist. Christians believe that human beings are very valuable because they are God's creations. But the non-Christian humanism we are now considering views humankind as occupying the ultimate position of authority.

This non-Christian kind of humanism is actually a very old viewpoint. It is commonly traced back to the ancient philosopher Protagoras. He espoused the *homo mensura* thesis: that humankind is "the measure of all things." Human beings are the ultimate judges—the only legitimate "measurers"—of what is good and true.

But we know that this perspective is even older than Protagoras. It goes back to the serpent in the Garden. "We can measure everything" is another way of saying, "We can be like God."

The 'Secular'

When people talk about this kind of humanism today they often give it a modifier: *secular* humanism. This is a helpful addition. It points to a specific way in which non-Christian people attempt to honor humanness.

What does *secular* mean? Some writers on the idea of the secular point to the slogan that appears on the U.S. dollar bill: *novus ordo seclorum*—"new order of the ages." Our word *secular* comes from the Latin word of which *sec(u)lorum* is a form. It refers to an "age" or a period of time.

In the past, Christians made frequent use of the word *secular*, and they did not give it bad connotations. *Secular* was a synonym for "temporal," in contrast to "eternal." For example, it has long been common practice for Roman Catholics to describe some priests as "secular." This means that they work in parishes, where they minister to Christians who are involved in "temporal" activities. This distinguishes them from "cloistered" clergy—people who live in monasteries, where they can concentrate more directly on eternal things.

Our present-day usage is connected to these past meanings. Today "secular" and "sacred" are still used to draw a contrast between the this-worldly and the otherworldly, between time and eternity.

What has changed in our day is that now "secular" has come to be associated with an "ism" that is opposed to the Christian way of viewing things.

Before looking more closely at this non-Christian perspective, let's try to be as clear as we can be on the good and the bad way of being in favor of the "secular." Strictly speaking, there is nothing objectionable, from a Christian point of view, in talking about a "secular" realm. We Christians believe that the world in which we live day to day is different from that heavenly realm where angels and departed saints experience eternal joy.

It is a common criticism of Christianity—the Marxists are especially fond of making this point—that we believers take refuge in a "pie-in-the-sky" religion. I am convinced that the best line of defense against this criticism is to respond along these lines: "Yes, that's true. In referring to a 'pie in the sky' you are obviously talking about our Christian belief in heaven. And we do believe in that. We Christians are on a journey to a better place. We are convinced that the pie really *is* in the sky."

To be sure, it would also be good to admit that a belief in heaven has often served as a poor excuse for ignoring the very real injustices that we encounter in this world. The God who is worshiped by angels in heaven cares deeply about what goes on in the earthly realm. It is bad theology to draw such rigid lines between the two realms that no relationship between them is acknowledged. When we serve God and neighbor in our everyday activities we are already relating to the "eternal."

But there is still a difference between heaven and earth. If *secular* is a way of referring to the affairs of this present world, it is a perfectly good term.

So why does the label have such a bad feel for Christians when it appears in *secular humanism*? Because in this pattern of thought the secular has become the fundamental reference point for understanding reality. The secular humanists preach the message that the secular is all that there is.

This view of reality is clearly stated in the "Humanist Manifesto II," a 1973 document that was endorsed by hundreds of academics, writers and artists, including Isaac Asimov, Betty Friedan, Sir Julian Huxley, and B. F. Skinner. "As nontheists," these self-proclaimed humanists declared, "we begin with humans not God, nature not deity. Nature may indeed be broader and deeper than we now know; any new discoveries, however, will but enlarge our knowledge of the natural."[1]

There is an interesting combination of open-mindedness and dogmatism in this statement of the humanist case. These humanists want to be open to the possibility that nature is "broader and deeper" than their present understanding indicates; they are willing to entertain surprises in their investigation of reality. But they do not expect to be startled out of their basic understanding of what reality is all about: "nature not deity" is where they begin—and they fully expect to end there as well.

It is easy, of course, for Christians to focus on the dogmatic rejection of belief in God. That is understandable—in ruling out the deity, these humanists are making a big leap.

But I need to repeat my observation that the "Manifesto" contains an interesting mix of both dogmatism and open-mindedness. If we are going to be fair to humanism we have to look at the open-mindedness as well.

Reductionism

In our attempt to be fair, let's take a brief look at some comments by Paul Kurtz, a leading proponent and organizer of the secular humanist cause. In his book of essays, *In Defense of Secular Humanism*, Kurtz frequently assures us that his perspective on reality is not "reductionist." He doesn't mean to "reduce" the world to a dull place from which all the creativity and mystery have been removed. What does this disavowal come to?

Kurtz wants a humanism that "takes seriously the diverse qualities encountered in human experience: in art, religion, morality, science, philosophy and ordinary life." He means to celebrate the rich variety of human existence. And he is willing to learn from any source—even traditional religion—that can help unlock our "creative capacities" and promote our "highest human excellences."[2]

Before going any further, let me say that I don't think Kurtz really does avoid reductionism. Indeed, he shows his hand in the very process of describing his open-mindedness. Whereas he wants a humanism that gives full play to the richness of human creativity, his perspective also "insists that these creative talents are fully describable as natural processes."[3]

Here is the basic reductionist conviction that inspires Kurtz's humanism. He wants to give play to the broadest "creative capacities" of the human spirit. He also wants to make room for all contributions—even religious ones—to the promotion of our "highest human excellences." But in the final analysis he still "insists" that all the data be "fully describable as natural processes."

Kurtz seems to be dogmatically committed to the thesis that everything that exists is contained within "nature." The "natural" encompasses everything. A God who exists beyond nature—and who is, indeed, the One on whom all natural things depend for their being—is not a serious possibility from Kurtz's point of view. This is surely a viewpoint that deserves to be called "reductionistic."

But if we stop there we will not be completely fair to Kurtz. Why does he make such a point of insisting that he is not reductionist in his thinking? Is he merely trying to be coy? Or is he engaged in conscious deception?

My guess is that Kurtz would admit that he is reductionistic in the sense that I claim he is. He would undoubtedly say that if we Christians want to label as reductionistic the hypothesis that everything that exists is encompassed by "nature," then he is a reductionist in that sense—he gladly accepts a picture of reality that is more "reduced" than the one that tries to populate the universe with gods and angels and devils and departed souls.

But Kurtz is also, in a significant sense, an opponent of various kinds of "reductionism." For example, he rejects the perspective of what he calls "the classical materialist," who treats the "variety and richness" of life as nothing but matter in motion. We must accept the real possibility, Kurtz insists, that nature has different "levels" built into it—and that we can't get rid of this variety of levels by trying to reduce nature to a single, uniform "block system."[4]

Kurtz wants to treat everything as "natural." In that sense he is a reductionist. But he is not happy with the way some other naturalists understand "nature." They sometimes try to squeeze all of the "natural" into very narrow molds. They won't allow nature to have its proper "variety and richness." In this sense Kurtz is a harsh critic of many kinds of reductionism.

Debates Among Humanists

Well, what is to be gained by this effort to be fair to secular humanists? Doesn't it needlessly complicate the picture? After all, we are agreed that in a basic and important sense Kurtz is a reductionist. He refuses to admit that anything exists outside the realm of "nature." And from a Christian point of view, that is an inadequate view of reality. Why go to the trouble, then, of pointing out that in another sense he is an opponent of certain varieties of reductionism?

One relevant answer is that it is unfair to Kurtz not to take his own criticisms of reductionism seriously. And as a conservative Protestant I have to admit that my kind of Christians don't deserve very high marks when it comes to fairness. We need practice at being fair to our adversaries. We can probably even afford to err in the direction of overdoing fairness for a while!

But that's to put the case in terms of courtesy. And as I said in an earlier chapter, listening carefully to our opponents is not simply good etiquette; we are also aiming at a deeper kind of self-improvement. We want to become more truthful Christians—truthful about ourselves and about others.

So let's try to think more expansively about being fair to secular humanists. How can we benefit from a more truthful evaluation of their views?

One thing we gain is the insights that they provide as they criticize each others' views. And let there be no doubt about the fact that they do engage in very intense criticism of each other.

To fail to see this is to ignore Satan's flexibility. The Devil, we noted earlier, is committed to one thing—getting people to trust in something other than the Creator. Outside of that he is quite open-minded.

Secular humanists respond to Satan's wiles by putting their basic trust in humanness. In making this choice they have zeroed in on one among many possibilities. They could have offered their allegiance to Baal or to Thor or to some African tribal deity. Or they could have worshiped the stars or the sun, or—as Augustine remarked—they could have acted very pious by choosing to worship the universe as a whole.

To be sure, in all these possible patterns of trust it is human pride that is at work. When people worship the sun, for example, they have decided that adoring the big ball of fire in the sky is more "manageable" religiously than bowing in humility before the Maker of the heavens and the earth.

The secular humanists have swept away many of the decorations that have often adorned other idolatries. They focus directly on the human itself, turning "You will be like God" into an explicit item of faith.

But even here—when humanness itself has been made the object of basic trust—even here there is flexibility. Suppose I decide to believe that the human person is "the measure of all things." I still have to decide what part or aspect of humanness does the "measuring."

For the sake of simplicity, let's take the three categories we mentioned earlier: the cognitive, the affective, and the volitional. Each of these can be treated as the basic "measuring" device in the human person.

The reality of these options was brought home to me in an argument that broke out between two students in a philosophy class I was teaching at a public university.

Alice and Harry were the most vocal class members. Alice was very enthusiastic about "the scientific method." For her, the detached weighing of evidence for and against a hypothesis was the only way to get at the truth about anything.

Harry was of a very different bent—a real "go with the flow" type. He was perfectly content to "kind of feel" his way through life. Beliefs and values were best decided, for Harry, on the basis of what you were "sort of comfortable with."

I did not preach at the class about my Christian convictions, but I didn't try to hide my faith commitment either. Neither Alice nor Harry were much taken with my religious orientation, and in a polite but animated way they let me know it on a regular basis.

One day Alice got going with her defense of "scientific objectivity," her target being people like me, who "accept things on faith." In the process of making her case she got in a few jabs at "subjectivity."

This set Harry's juices to flowing. "Why does it always have to be such a head trip with you, Alice?" he complained. "Can't you ever just let it happen? Don't you ever just *feel*?" Harry's "just feeling" immediately loomed as a bigger sin in Alice's mind than my "just trusting"; she took after his "mindless emotions" with glee. And with equal fervor Harry countered with his own worries about her "insistence on intellectualizing everything."

As I witnessed this lively discussion between two bright students I was struck by how much they really did disagree with each other. Yet each of them was a "secular humanist." Each believed that all of reality is contained within "nature," or the "secular" realm. And each believed that—within the all-encompassing sphere of the natural—the human person is the measure of all things.

Where they disagreed was on this question: What is the best way of doing the measuring? Alice was convinced that we should engage in cognitive measuring; we are at our human best when we are "objectively" weighing the scientific evidence. But Harry sees Alice's means of deciding the issues as much too restrictive. He advocates affective measuring. We can only make healthy choices when we are "really in touch with our feelings."

And it is not difficult to imagine a third voice entering the intra-humanist debate—the proponent of volitional measuring. Let's try to hear this voice: "The important thing is to make your own choice. You, Alice, have decided to be a scientifically oriented person. And you, Harry, have opted for subjective feelings. Neither of these is 'wrong' in itself. Each of you has to see that we don't 'have' to be either objective or subjective. We can choose to follow one or the other, or we can choose to combine them. What is important to recognize is that behind every belief and value there is a will that has *chosen* to make that belief or value an important one."

The humanists have genuine arguments with each other. People can agree with each other that the human person is the highest authority in the universe, yet they can still differ about how human beings best go about exercising that authority. Indeed, the disagreements can get even more complicated than I have indicated here. But we need not go into all of the complexities. The important thing is to recognize that the arguments are genuine—and they cut deep.

Applying the Lessons to Ourselves

This would be an opportune time to play the divide-and-conquer game. That's a tactic that is often effective in winning battles, especially intellectual battles. You get your opponents to start arguing with each other and wait until they use up valuable resources on internal squabbling—then you move in for the kill.

But we need to avoid that temptation here. Our primary goal is not to win but to understand. That is not to say that we don't care about winning the arguments; we certainly want to be on the victorious side in the larger cosmic battle against Satan. As Christians, though, we don't want to separate understanding from winning. Or to phrase it differently: the best way to win the battle for truth is to concentrate on truth rather than winning.

When we say that secular humanists are divided among themselves, then, we aren't trying to gain a cheap debater's advantage. Our point is not to exult in their disunity. "See? They can't even make up their own minds about how to 'measure'! Behold how they hate one another!" To pursue the discussion in that spirit would not be a great advance over the habit of treating secular humanism as one monolithic conspiracy of evil.

The truth of the matter is that it would be hypocritical for Christians to taunt the secular humanists for their disunity. We have similar disunity within our own ranks.

I don't mean to rehearse here all the standard complaints about denominational and theological divisions in the Christian community. I'm thinking of differences among Christians that closely approximate the intrahumanist arguments about measuring.

We Christians have our own "measuring" debates. And they are important debates, so important, I suggest, that we would do well to learn what we can from the arguments the humanists conduct among themselves.

But isn't it odd to suggest that Christians can have a trouble with the measuring question? How can that be? Don't we give a very different answer to the question about "the measure of all things"? Isn't our answer this: *God* is the measure of all things? And if that *is* our answer, can't we just ignore the question about which dimension of our humanness does the basic measuring?

Yes, we do give a different answer to the basic measuring question. And, yes, our answer is indeed that the ultimate measurer is God. But that doesn't mean that we can completely avoid discussions about how we human beings should do our measuring.

The debates among Christians get going when we think about how God gets through to us. When we receive God's guidance for our lives, which part of us does the primary "receiving"?

This may seem like an abstract issue at first blush. But it really isn't. Let me illustrate the point by imagining three Christian voices in which we hear similar tones to those that resound in the intrahumanist debates.

First voice: "I can't emphasize enough the importance of sound doctrine. Satan gets hold of us by convincing us of a false view of reality. We must oppose him by articulating a correct view of things. God gave us his infallible word, the Bible, as a system of true teachings, so that we will not be tossed to and fro by every wind of doctrine that comes our way."

Second voice: "Head-knowledge is not nearly as important as heart-knowledge. The Devil knows all the true doctrines, but that kind of learning cannot save him! The all-important thing is to feel the truth in our inner being. God reaches into our lives by granting us a peace and a joy that the world could never give us.

How do I know that I am on the road to heaven? I experience it in the deepest recesses of my soul!"

Third voice: "Neither doctrine nor inner experience is the place to begin. Think of all the slave-owners who had all the 'right' beliefs and felt 'peace and joy' in their souls. Yet they were vicious racists! It's not what we think or what we feel; it's what we will to be and to do. Each of us is called to choose a pattern of living, Christian discipleship. When we have made that choice, our thoughts and feelings will fall into line."

Admittedly, these examples are a bit simple. We can imagine variations on each of these voices. But these three are enough to show that the respective roles of thinking, feeling, and choosing in the Christian life are matters of lively debate.

I'm not going to try to settle the intra-Christian debate here. Actually, I don't think any permanent "settlement" is possible for Christians.

For one thing, I don't see any of the three candidates—the cognitive, the affective and the volitional—as *the* primary factor in our relationship to God. We humans have been made with the capacity for trust. And it is in that space where we form our deepest trustings—the intimate place that the Bible calls "the heart"—that we find our real center as human creatures. This trusting-space is more basic than our cognition or affection or volition. It is where direction is given to our thinking, feeling, and choosing. So I am arguing for the primacy of the heart. The other three factors are not as basic—even though some Christians tend to treat the "heart" as the "feeling" place.

Suppose we agree, then, that the heart is our centering space, and that thought, feeling, and will are secondary aspects of our nature. That doesn't mean that these other three aspects aren't an important part of who we are! We must still find a proper recipe for putting them together in our lives.

There may not be a single recipe, though, that applies uniformly to all people. It is quite plausible to argue, I think, that once each of us has settled the basic trust relationship in the right way, the other factors may be put together in different combinations and with varying doses. How we mix cognition, affect and volition in our individual lives is something we decide with reference to our personal callings and gifts.

But it is a good thing also to think in general terms about how these three factors can relate to each other. Let's pursue the recipe analogy a bit further. There is no single "right" recipe for an apple pie; different combinations of ingredients can produce equally satisfactory results. But it still important to know about healthy ingredients and about potentially disastrous combinations.

The analogy should be clear. Christians do need to think about the general ways of combining the cognitive, the affective, and the volitional. And we can learn something, I suggest, from secular humanists' arguments about the role these ingredients play in human lives.

Our Humanist Teachers?

But suppose a stubborn questioner pushes me on this last point: granted that we need to think about the recipe—can we really learn anything important from the secular humanists on the subject? Why should we expect them to have anything legitimate to teach us?

These are good questions. A few answers are in order.

The secular humanists are working with excellent material. I overheard two college students talking about their studies. One mentioned the name of her instructor in English literature. The other student interrupted: "How can you stand to be in his class? He's so boring! The first student replied: "But he is talking about such interesting writings—even *he* can't completely mess up that kind of material!"

That's also what we have to say about the secular humanists' discussions of human nature. No matter how wrong-headed their basic approach is, even *they* can't completely mess up that kind of material! In focusing on human nature they are dealing with the crowning glory of God's creating activity. Given the subject matter, it would be surprising if nothing of the created splendor shone through.

Secular humanists often uncover special features of their subject matter. There's an old wisecrack about paranoids that goes something like this: it's good to have at least one paranoid for a friend, just in case somebody really *is* out to get you. Paranoids usually fret about conspiracies that aren't really there, but they are also more likely than most of us to hit upon any real conspiracies that happen to be in the air.

Remember, Satan's big lie is a distorted truth. Like paranoia, it blows things way out of proportion. Sinful theories about reality regularly take hold of something that is in itself a God-created good and then proceed to treat this good something as if it were the most important thing that exists, the most reliable dimension of reality.

Thus the various manifestations of secular humanism. The secular humanist takes hold of that glorious stuff called human nature and proclaims it to be the highest authority in the cosmos. Then some aspect of human consciousness—thinking, feeling, choosing—is identified as the supreme "measure of all things."

Let me say it bluntly, just so I am not misunderstood: this is bad, wicked, perverse. But none of that detracts from the fact that the humanists are working with good materials. And in the very practice of concentrating too much on one aspect of reality, the secular humanists often manage to take an extremely close look at something that is a part of the good world that God made.

Consider a simple example. Suppose we meet a humanist who has adopted a rather unnuanced version of behaviorism. This person is convinced that human beings are nothing more than complex physical organisms who are reacting to environmental stimuli.

"I'm not interested in your fictions about 'the soul' or 'the inner life,'" such a person says. "We are physical beings who respond to our physical environments. My so-called subjective life is nothing but behaviors that I have learned in order to cope with environmental stimuli. If we don't like the way people act, then our only hope is to alter the environment that has conditioned us. That's what science is equipped to do—to study our environment and recommend those changes that will bring about more harmonious behaviors."

Presented as a comprehensive account of the human condition, this viewpoint is clearly unsatisfactory. But that doesn't mean it has nothing to teach us.

Scholars who accepted this behaviorist perspective would go out of their way to link specific human "behaviors" with "environmental stimuli." If they came across someone who was afraid that God might send him or her to hell, for example, these scholars would try to explain this fearful behavior in terms of "negative conditioning" in that person's childhood—some children come to expect punishment whenever they act in certain ways.

Now, this does not satisfy me as a general explanation of the belief in hell. If you believe in a God who hates sin, then hell is not something that can be psychologized away.

There are some people, though, whose fear of hell does have much to do with childhood experiences. And we defenders of doctrinal orthodoxy aren't always as sensitive to these influences as we should be. We would do well, then, to check in with the behaviorists every so often. Like the paranoids, they might be discovering real plots that the rest of us could easily miss!

Secular humanists can help us to see our own shortcomings. One of my seminary students made an interesting comment about the various manifestos and declarations collected in Paul Kurtz's *In Defense of Secular Humanism*. "When I was reading this stuff it struck me that so much attention was given to attacking religion and defending sex," she reported. "But then it occurred to me that these secular humanists are probably doing this because they see us as always defending religion and attacking sex!"

My guess is that she has a good grasp of what is going on in the humanist psyche. Kurtz's book is full of references to the stifling influence of religion—and sexuality is what people complain most about when they talk about how religion takes the fun out of life.

Aren't the secular humanists just rationalizing their own sinful desires when they complain about religion and sex? Maybe. But that does not mean that there is no truth in their complaints. People can say true things even when they are motivated by a desire to cover up their own sins.

Suppose a man has committed adultery, and, in order to hide the seriousness of what he has done, he makes all sorts of accusations against his wife—she's insensitive, unloving, and self-centered. We know that he is engaging in rationalization. His basic problem is that he has been an unfaithful husband. But that doesn't rule out the possibility that some of his accusations against her are on target. Indeed, a fair assessment of their marriage may well have to address the very faults he has identified.

Secular humanists may have all the wrong motives in criticizing Christian thought and practice. But they still do on occasion zero in on genuine defects in the Christian community.

A gay activist once wrote that describing homosexuals as "faggots" originated in the medieval period. When a town wanted to start a bonfire, they would round up known homosexuals and use them as kindling—fagots—to light the fire.

I don't know whether this is historically accurate, but it wouldn't surprise me if it were. My views about what the Bible teaches regarding homosexuality are conservative. No one would cheer if I proclaimed them at a gay-lesbian support rally. But I am also convinced that Christians have been inexcusably cruel to homosexual persons. We have treated them in ways that no human beings deserve to be treated.

You don't have to be a friend of the sexual revolution to know that the Christian record of dealing with sexual matters is nothing to celebrate. Nor do you have to be a free thinker to admit that the church has often squelched creative intellectual inquiry. Nor do you have to be a radical feminist to see that the Christian community has not always allowed women to realize their God-given potentials.

Christians have no business being arrogant with secular humanists about the role of religion in human life. We know that we are sinners, and we should be willing to confess publicly that our secular humanist opponents are often perceptive about our shortcomings.

Our Christian argument with secular humanism is a many-sided one. Or more precisely: it is an ongoing discussion that includes a number of different arguments. Sometimes the arguments will be between different factions within the secular humanist camp. It is good to listen carefully to these exchanges. Sometimes we will even find ourselves siding with one or another secular humanist viewpoint as a specific point is being debated.

We would do well to keep listening even when the arguments are directed toward our own thoughts and practices. Secular humanists are wrong in their views about God. They are often quite perceptive, however, in their assessments of *us*.

But we need to do more than listen to secular humanists. We also need to engage them in dialogue by responding to their formulations.

We need not be reluctant to assure the secular humanists that we see ourselves as participating with them in a joint investigation. The subject matter they have chosen to make the centerpiece of their intellectual inquiry is something to which we are also deeply committed. We too want to celebrate the value of being human.

The secular humanists are wrong to proclaim that humankind is the supreme "measure of all things." But in turning human nature into a false god they have indeed directed their attention to that which is God-*like*. Human persons are unique creations, fashioned with special affection by the Creator of the heavens and the earth.

We will not have served our humanist neighbors well if we simply denounce their views in a spirit of arrogance. Better to give humble testimony to the grace that empowers us to confess our own errors and shortcomings, in the hope that we may yet gain new opportunities to bear witness to the Bible's portrayal of the created worth—and the profound mystery—of our humanness.

5. How to Avoid Merging with the One

I always enjoy introducing unsuspecting students to the philosophy of Parmenides, a Greek thinker who lived during the first half of the fifth century B.C. Parmenides was a metaphysical monist. To say that his view was "metaphysical" is to identify it as a theory about the nature of reality. And to call his metaphysics "monist" is to say that he was a "one-ist."

All reality, Parmenides insisted, is made up of only one kind of stuff. And as he viewed the situation, the one stuff of which everything is composed is Being—or What Is.

On the face of things, that may not seem to be such an odd notion. Certainly the idea that everything in the cosmos participates in What Is probably won't strike most ordinary folks as a deeply repugnant proposal. If a philosopher is going to insist that everything is made up of a single kind of stuff, then What Is seems to be a more plausible candidate for status as the basic metaphysical substance than, say, peanut butter or Elmer's glue.

But Parmenides pushed his metaphysical monism in a rather surprising direction. And he argued his case in a very clever fashion.

All he asks us to accept at the outset of the discussion is this formulation: What Is, is; and What Is Not, is not. But from this seemingly innocent proposition, Parmenides draws some rather shocking conclusions. He argues, for example, that What Is cannot be divided, nor can it move. Suppose, argues Parmenides, that What Is *could* be divided. What is it, then, that would separate one piece of What Is from another? Well, it would either have to be a portion of What Is Not or a portion of What Is. But if it is What Is Not that is standing between two pieces of What Is, then wouldn't we have to say that a parcel of What Is Not is separating the two What Is segments? But this would be to say that What Is Not *is*—and we have already agreed that What Is, is; and What Is Not, is not. Therefore, only What Is can stand between two pieces of What Is. And this is to say that there is really no break at all: What Is is one continuous and undivided Being.

Or suppose What Is could move. Where would it move to? To What Is Not? If so, then it would be proper to say that What Is Not *is* the place to which What Is moves. But What Is Not cannot be a place that *is*—since we have agreed that What Is, is; and What Is Not, is not.

Parmenides wasn't just playing silly word games. He was setting forth a serious theory about the nature of reality. He was meaning to tell us about the way it all is: what we call "the universe" is in fact unchanging, unmoving, undifferentiated Being.

But don't we experience change and movement and diversity in our world? We certainly *seem* to. And Parmenides is eager to warn us against putting too much stock in what "seems" to be. Appearances are deceiving. Indeed, even the deep conviction that most of us have that we human beings are distinct centers of consciousness—this too is an illusion. Being is a single thing, pure and unmixed What Is, the One.

Contemporary Monism

With the right sort of promotion, Parmenides could sell a lot of books in the twentieth century. In fact, Richard Bach's bestselling novel *One* is in effect a contemporary updating of Parmenides' philosophy. Bach's story is a fictionalized account of the spiritual journey that he and his wife, Leslie, have been pursuing in their life together. Actually, Richard Bach tells us, he and Leslie wrote the book together. Indeed, in a profound sense they do *everything* together: "We've become RiLeschardlie, no longer knowing where one of us ends and the other begins."[1]

But it isn't just the boundaries of their own interpersonal relationship that have become blurred for "RiLeschardlie." They have discovered that there really is only one life in the whole universe. Everything is one grand, cosmic, loving person.

They illustrate this spiritual discovery by spinning out an allegory of a airplane journey that they take together. On this pilgrimage they visit their own earlier selves, and along the way they encounter the unhappy selves that they might have been had they not chosen to give themselves to each other with total abandon.

The Bachs also discover that "humanness" is a much larger reality than they had once thought. In the course of their travels they encounter a computer named Mashara, who seems also to be caught up in the business of loving. Are you alive? they ask her. Is that so unthinkable? she responds; can't humanity shine forth from the atoms of a machine as well as those that make up human flesh? "Humanity isn't a physical description," the Bachs are instructed, "it's a spiritual goal."[2]

The "RiLeschardlie" team finally discovers that we are all aspects of each other. And when we truly love, we are lifted above space and time. All that we associate with a sense of past and present, here and there, fades away.

Like Parmenides, then, the Bachs believe that What Is is an undifferentiated unity. The appearance of diversity is a deception. By allowing ourselves to be caught up in love, we experience the only true reality: oneness.

Monistic Variety

Monisms come in different brands and doses. And before saying more about the Parmenidean kind of monism, and its contemporary attractiveness for people like Leslie and Richard Bach, we must take a closer look at the very idea of a monistic outlook.

To qualify as a monist you have to think that it is important to emphasize the "oneness" of everything. But, of course, you might disagree with other monists about the nature of that oneness. One *what?* That is the question every serious monist must answer.

Parmenides was content to specify the one as Being, or What Is. The views of "RiLeschardlie" seem to lean in a more spiritual direction; for them, What Is seems to be a cosmic consciousness or an undifferentiated Loving.

It is possible, though, to espouse versions of monism very different from these. Indeed, secular humanism is a kind of monism. Secular humanists insist that everything is contained within "nature." And this means—and I am thinking here of those secular humanists who put their basic trust in scientific reasoning—that all of reality is made up of that which is studied by the scientists.

A century ago, the proponents of a secular humanist type of perspective would have said that everything is made up of "matter." But "matter" is a less useful term in scientific discussions today. It is not so easy to think of phenomena like kinetic energy and magnetic fields as "matter in motion." Secular humanists today often prefer labels like "physicalism" or "naturalism" over the older "materialism."

Whatever terminology the secular humanists choose, though, they are united in what they deny. There is nothing over and above "nature." All of reality is made up of the kind of stuff that the sciences are capable of explaining.

This denial that there is more than one level of reality, or more than one kind of basic stuff, is essential to monism in all its forms. And it is helpful to keep that fact in mind: when monists of all varieties insist that there is basically only one kind of stuff in the universe, they are challenging the view that there is more than one stuff. Typically, they are reacting against some kind of dualism.

Metaphysical dualism is the view that reality is made up of two kinds of stuff. The philosopher Plato is easily the most prominent of all dualistic thinkers in the history of this subject. He taught that there are two very different levels of reality; these two levels display two irreducibly differing metaphysical substances: the physical and the spiritual. The former is the realm of time, the latter of eternity.

In Plato's scheme, human beings bridge these two levels. Our bodies belong to the physical world, our souls to the spiritual or intelligible realm. Obviously, this dualistic view of human beings in particular, and of reality in general, has had an immense influence in Western thought.

Monists are typically people who dislike the dualistic picture of things. When they say, "One," they are usually mumbling under their breath, "Not two!"

But if you are going to whittle Plato's twoness down to a oneness, you have to decide which one of Plato's two stuffs you are going to favor. Thus there are spiritualizing monists and physicalizing monists. Scientifically oriented secular humanists are physicalizers: all reality falls within the domain of the "natural." "RiLeschardlie," on the other hand, opts for a spiritual monism: it may appear that machines are made of metal and we are made of meat, but if the truth were known, the Bachs tells us, we are all mere aspects of a unified, timeless, spiritual Loving.

Different Doses

Monisms also come in different doses. For our purposes we can think of strong and weak monisms. A strong monism says that there really is only one thing in the universe, and the appearance of "manyness" is an illusion. That's the Parmenides-"RiLeschardlie" perspective.

The eighteenth-century British philosopher George Berkeley had a weaker kind of monistic view. He denied the reality of matter as a kind of stuff that exists independently of spirit. Berkeley argued that the only things that exist are minds and their ideas: what we call material objects are really bundles of mental impressions.

His view, then, was a spiritualistic, or mentalistic, monism. But though Berkeley held that the mental is the only real stuff, he did not insist that there is only one great big Mind. He believed that there are many minds: God's mind, Berkeley's mind, the queen's mind, and so on. And these many minds are, in turn, filled with all sorts of different ideas. For Berkeley, mental reality is very rich and diverse.

Berkeley's perspective is an example of a weak monism. There is, on such a view, one *kind* of stuff, with the diversity of the universe being held together by a uniform metaphysical substance. But there is, nonetheless, a real diversity. The appearance of many-ness is no illusion.

The naturalizing secular humanists are also weak monists. They don't deny the diversity of things in the universe. But they do insist that everything that does exist, in all of its manyness and richness, is made up of the same physical substance.

The Crusade Against Monism

It will be helpful to keep these monistic variations in mind as we think about the relationship between Christianity and monism. But we're especially interested here in the spiritualizing variety of monism, the kind that comes in the strong dose prescribed by "RiLeschardlie."

What's going on in this fascination with metaphysical oneness? And how should we evaluate this urge to be absorbed into a cosmic unity?

These questions have been receiving considerable attention in the Christian community in recent years. Many of the Christians who joined "the battle for the mind" against secular humanism have subsequently enlarged their campaign by attacking spiritualizing monism, especially as these monistic impulses took shape in the "New Age" movement. Many of these Christians have expressed their concerns in an alarmist fashion, attacking New Age monists with the same crusading intensity that they have displayed in opposing secular humanism.

Much of their distress is understandable. In each case—in the struggles against secular humanism and against the New Age movement—the Christian crusaders have been especially concerned about the influence of these philosophies on educational systems. And they are correct in thinking that each of these two perspectives has had a significant influence upon educational practice.

They are also correct in perceiving that New Age teachings have displaced secular humanist themes in certain segments of the population. Much of the New Age movement is in effect a rejection of secular humanist ideas. Many of our contemporaries have turned to a spiritualizing monism because they have sensed that naturalistic reasoning cannot deliver satisfactory answers to the "big" issues of life.

But Christian attacks on New Age thinking have not always been discerning about the character of the monistic yearning for cosmic unities. This is not to say that Christians are wrong in judging the quest for the One to be a sinful project; it is. And the sinful desire to be absorbed into What Is certainly must be exposed and criticized from the perspective of biblical Christianity. But the Christian alarmists have not shown much of a willingness to think about "the hopes and fears" that are at work in contemporary monism.

Monism and Scientific Technology

The New Age as an identifiable movement may not turn out to be an enduring presence on the North American scene. But the monism that has been an important feature of this movement is certainly no passing fad. New Age monism has tapped into some deep impulses in contemporary life. And it is important for Christians to understand these impulses if we are going to explain to our contemporaries how the gospel speaks to "the hopes and fears of all the years."

What about the monistic impulse, then? What is going on when people are caught up in a quest for oneness?

Let me make it clear again that I agree with the Christian crusaders in their insistence that the monistic impulse is a sinful one. The promise that we can be absorbed into a cosmic oneness is another version of the serpent's lie. In an important sense, spiritualizing monism is one more perverse strategy in the "you will be like God" game.

Here again, though, the serpent's untruth is not simply a blatant falsehood; it is a distorted truth. The promise of oneness is a twisted version of something that God really does want for his human creatures. It would be wrong simply to reject out of hand everything that the spiritualizing monists say by way of defending their views.

Monism is attractive to many of our contemporaries because they see it as a corrective to what they experience as the defects of secular humanism. For one thing, some people aren't very happy about living in a world that seems to be dominated by scientific technology. I once talked to a computer programmer who told me that when he had to make really important decisions he consulted astrological charts. I asked him how he reconciled a trust in astrology with his own sophisticated training in scientific technology. His response: "I haven't really thought much about that. But I sure wouldn't want to live in a world where we engineering types ran the whole show!"

This man was instinctively reaching out for something that would place limits on scientific technology. He was well trained in physics, but he was not happy about living in a universe that is completely defined by the science.

Some New Age thinkers have followed through on this sense of dissatisfaction by arguing that we need a "new physics." Fritjof Capra is a guru of the New Age movement who is well known for the way he makes the case for a new, and more mystical, scientific outlook. Capra doesn't ask us to reject the scientific study of reality as such. Instead he argues for a new way of envisioning the scientific quest. He proposes, for example, that the study of nuclear physics should be viewed as an encounter with "the cosmic dance of energy."[3]

The "energy" Capra is talking about here is spiritual in nature. He is rejecting the notion that when scientists look at objects under microscopes they are getting closer to a reality that consists of matter in motion. We must do away with this older notion that the basic constituents of reality are distinct and impersonal atoms. This "atomistic" conception of reality has to give way to the view that everything is ultimately a manifestation of spiritual energy. We are all caught up—all of us: people, animals, plants, and artifacts—in the "cosmic dance" of the One.

Again, Capra isn't rejecting science as such. But he is proposing a whole new way of viewing the reality that scientists study.

Monism and Connectedness

Just as spiritualizing monism is a protest against an impersonal "atomistic" account of our nonhuman environment, so it is also a rejection of a social "atomism."

The oft-quoted lines, "No man is an island / No man stands alone," were penned a few centuries ago by the poet John Donne. The present-day monists are offering a very strong endorsement to Donne's sentiment. We human beings are not isolated "atoms." We are held together by strong bonds, so strong that it is fair to say that ultimately we are really all One.

Before we become too critical of the monists on this point, we must admit that they are challenging a very dangerous trend in recent times. In 1979, Christopher Lasch published his much-discussed book *The Culture of Narcissism*, in which he argued that the American "pursuit of happiness" has finally arrived at "the dead end of a narcissistic preoccupation with the self."[4] The popular self-help literature of the 1970s provided abundant evidence for the kind of narcissistic tendencies that Lasch was criticizing. "Finding yourself," "being *you*," "doing your own thing"—these were common themes in best-selling therapy manuals. People were being encouraged to view themselves as isolated little "atoms"—or "islands"—of selfish pleasure.

Consider, for example, Fritz Perls's much displayed little manifesto, which he perversely entitled the "Gestalt Prayer":

I do my thing, and you do your thing.
I am not in this world to live up to your expectations.
And you are not in this world to live up to mine.
You are you, and I am I.
And if by chance we find each other, it's beautiful.
If not, it can't be helped.[5]

Contemporary monism is a firm rejection of this picture of human selfhood. The people who are attracted to monistic views of reality are trying to find each other; *networking* and *connecting* are important words in the New Age vocabulary.

Remember the Bachs' allegorical account of their high-flying journey? They are ecstatic about coming to a point in their travels together where they can no longer separate out their individual pilgrimages. This is surely a far cry from Perls's "I do my thing, and you do your thing."

Indeed, not only have the Bachs' individual consciousnesses begun to merge into a single "RiLeschardlie," but the two of them now suspect that this is only a first step toward a much grander kind of merger toward which they and everything else are headed. It is not enough just to "network" with a few other people; the aim is to experience the universe itself as a vast network of unifying energy. Joining the cosmic "dance" is the ultimate in "connecting"!

Christians and Dualism

We have already noted that monists are especially upset about dualism. They are strong anti-Platonists. Plato insisted that reality was separated into two different kinds of being. It isn't difficult to see why contemporary monists would reject Platonism. They want to get rid of all those pictures of reality that posit permanent divisions in the order of things.

As a Christian, I share some of their hostility toward Platonistic dualism. I agree that Plato's dualist scheme has done a lot of harm in Western culture.

It is unfortunate, for example, that many Christians have

assumed that Plato's views about spirit and matter are very close to the way the Bible portrays the nature of reality. They have thought that when the Bible refers to the struggle between "flesh" and "spirit" it is encouraging us to elevate nonphysical activities, such as contemplating abstractions and working geometric proofs and longing to get rid of our bodies, over eating pizza and fixing dripping faucets and hugging our children.

This is misguided. The biblical categories don't cover exactly the same territory as Plato's. In Galatians 5, for example, Paul tells us that "envy" is one of the "works of the flesh," while "gentleness" is one of the "fruits of the Spirit." A geometrician is being "fleshly," then, when he or she is envious of a colleague's ability to work the proofs faster. And a father's gentle rocking of his baby daughter can count as a very "spiritual" activity.

The adoption of a strongly Platonistic notion of a human person as a lofty eternal spirit temporarily inhabiting an inferior physical receptacle has had unfortunate effects in a number of areas of human interaction. It has given us the wrong picture of the place of sexuality in our lives, for example. And it has reinforced the idea that occupations that require mental skills are "holier" than those that require a high degree of physical exertion. Christians should be wary of many ideas that are associated with metaphysical dualism. New Age thinking, along with other manifestations of monism, directs our attention to some important questions. We ought to be grateful to a movement that forces us to come to a clearer understanding of what it means to be a well-integrated human being.

But no Christian can really be against dualism as such. In one extremely important sense, Christian thought is inescapably and non-negotiably dualistic. A dualist says that in the final analysis reality divides into two categories. And in the final analysis that is exactly what the Bible teaches.

But this is not to say that the Bible issues a straightforward endorsement of Plato's kind of dualism. The basic duality in the biblical scheme is not spirit and matter. In the biblical scheme of things the fundamental twoness that simply cannot be avoided has to do with the crucial distinction between the Creator and the creation.

To deny this dualism is the basic sin. This is why the biblical writers spend so much time warning us against idolatry—which is treating something creaturely as if it has the ultimacy that belongs only to God. God is God. And the creaturely is the creaturely. Those may seem to be such simple assertions that they hardly need to be emphasized. But ever since the Fall, our basic confusion has stemmed from an inability to keep them straight.

Downgrading the Creator

There are different strategies available for confusing the Creator with the creation. One very basic ploy is to downgrade the Creator. Another one is to upgrade the creation.

Secular humanists attempt the first ploy. They try to bring God down to earth, so to speak.

Obviously that's not the way the secular humanists themselves would describe what they are doing. They would more likely claim that they have simply gotten rid of God. Christians think there are two kinds of reality: God and the universe. Secular humanists eliminate God. All that is left is the universe. And secular humanism is quite content with that state of affairs.

But it isn't really that simple. You can't just eliminate God and keep the universe the way it was. Something of what used to belong to God now has to be poured into the universe.

Consider the question of authority. In the Creator-plus-the-creation worldview that the secularists reject, God is the source of authoritative guidance. The divine will is the ultimate reference point for deciding what is good and just and beautiful and true. If you want to get rid of the divine will, you will still need some sort of reference point for dealing with these issues. People—even secular humanist people—still want to find answers to questions about goodness and justice and beauty and truth. Those sorts of questions don't just go away once you stop believing that there is a divine Creator.

The authoritative center will now have to be located within the universe. And when we pour that kind of authority into the world, our conception of the world itself changes. The world takes on a kind of ultimacy that it did not have before.

The *study* of the world also takes on a new character under this secularist regime. From within a biblical worldview, science can function in a rather modest fashion. We can study the way things are in order to try to figure out how they work. But we Christians realize that only God *really* knows how things work. So our efforts at explanation will be humble attempts to think some of God's thoughts after him, knowing full well that our formulations will be, at best, mere approximations to the divine wisdom.

But when human scientific rationality becomes the ultimate standard of truth, the study of the universe takes on a new kind of significance. Science becomes our best shot at coming up with the answers to life's most important questions.

And this will end up requiring some sort of squeezing or deflating. If the answers that scientific rationality comes up with don't seem to be "big" enough to match the scope of our humanness, then our humanness will inevitably get whittled down.

B. F. Skinner's perspective is a good case in point here. In his book *Beyond Freedom and Dignity,* he argued that, given our scientific understanding of reality, the old notion that human beings have a natural (created) freedom and dignity has become outmoded. His title embodies his prescription: we have to get "beyond" these notions. Unfortunately, though, "beyond" here really means "beneath." For Skinner, the notions of freedom and dignity are too exalted a way of characterizing the likes of us. His own preferred way of organizing human reality is to allow scientific technology to control our conditioned responses. This will produce a harmonious environment in which we are all happier.

But secular humanism will inevitably fail to deliver on its promises. That may seem like a very smug thing for a Christian to say. And we Christians always do run the risk of sounding smug when we talk about these issues. Smugness is a self-satisfied attitude. In intellectual discussion, it often takes the form of an "I'm right and you're wrong" dogmatism or an "I told you so!" kind of sneering triumphalism.

That's not the spirit I mean to encourage when I say that secular humanism will inevitably fail to deliver on its promises. I do mean to suggest, though, that if we accept as true a Christian conviction that a great gap exists between Creator and creation, the attempt to attribute ultimacy to something other than the Creator is bound to fall short of success. From a Christian point of view, neither the world nor the scientific study of the world can handle that kind of ultimacy. That's too much baggage for a creation to have to carry.

So when we Christians see our fellow human beings accepting a secular humanist perspective, we have good reasons to expect disillusionment to set in eventually.

And that is exactly what is happening in the recent upsurge of spiritualizing monism. People have become dissatisfied with the kind of secular humanist perspective that insists that we put our basic trust in scientific rationality.

Upgrading the Creation

The seekers after the One have opted for the second of the two ploys I mentioned earlier. Unlike the secular humanists, who have tried to downgrade the Creator, they have attempted to upgrade the creation. Instead of trying to squeeze something of the divine into a naturalistically understood universe, they are intent upon lifting up the universe into the divine. Rather than secularizing the divine, we might say, they want to "divinize" the secular.

Earlier I noted that New Age thinkers don't denounce science as such. Instead, they call for a new way of looking at the scientific enterprise. This is important to keep in mind. The kind of spiritualizing monism that we encounter these days is not simply a throwback to earlier, pre-scientific ways of viewing the world. The monists see themselves as pushing the scientific quest to a new stage of awareness.

Spiritualizing monism need not be seen, then, as a radical break with the Enlightenment outlook that shaped secular humanism. The historian Henry May has suggested that Enlightenment thought is based on these two propositions: "first, that the present age is more enlightened than the past; and second, that we understand nature and man best through the use of our natural faculties."[6]

Today's spiritualizing monists would not so much reject these propositions as they would insist on new ways of understanding them. To be properly "enlightened" today, they would argue, is to get past the restrictive categories of secular humanism. Evolution — the process that has been so important to the defenders of scientific rationality — is actually taking us beyond the atomistic physicalism of the older ways of studying reality. And this means, in turn, that we are gaining a new sense of how to understand and exercise "our natural faculties." The possibilities of humanness are breaking out of the old molds — into new "connections"!

The spiritualizing monists want to preserve something of the older sense of divinity. They want a realm of exalted being that is high and lifted up, permeated with mystery, resplendent with glory and wisdom.

And here's the twist: they want *us* to occupy that realm.

Of course, they know that, given the shape we're in at present, we humans aren't exactly ready to sit on heaven's throne. But they insist that we are quite capable of moving in that direction — especially if we do so collectively, by working together to achieve new levels of transpersonal consciousness. And in attaining these new levels of human awareness, we will serve as the avante garde of reality as such, as we move to a consciousness that encompasses even more than the human. By working to achieve a sense of unity with what we have for so long thought of as "mere nature," we can bring the whole of physical reality with us into an undifferentiated oneness.

In Praise of Manyness

G. K. Chesterton regularly took up the cudgels against the spiritualizing monists of his day. One of his favorite targets was

Annie Besant, a leader in England's theosophy movement around the turn of this century. Mrs. Besant worked actively to bring about religious unity. There can really be only one religion, she argued, since we are all parts of a single universal Self. And how can a single universal Self actually believe contradictory dogmas?

Chesterton scoffed at this notion that "we are really all one person." His response is worth quoting at length:

> According to Mrs. Besant . . . there are no real walls of individuality between man and man. If I may put it so, she does not tell us to love our neighbours; she tells us to be our neighbours. . . . And I never heard of any suggestion in my life with which I more violently disagree. I want to love my neighbour not because he is I, but precisely because he is not. I want to adore the world, not as one likes a looking-glass, because it is one's self, but as one loves a woman, because she is entirely different. If souls are separate love is possible. If souls are united love is obviously impossible. A man may be said loosely to love himself, but he can hardly fall in love with himself, or, if he does, it must be a monotonous courtship. If the world is full of real selves, they can be really unselfish selves. But upon Mrs. Besant's principle the whole cosmos is only one enormously selfish person.[7]

This is a helpful argument. According to the way the Bible pictures What Is, reality is characterized by fundamental plurality, a plurality that is so basic to the way things are that we can never get rid of it. We have to learn to respect it. And even that is not quite enough. We can also learn to rejoice in it.

First, we can rejoice in the basic duality between Creator and creature. Chesterton describes this state of affairs succinctly: Christianity teaches, he observes, that "this separation between God and man is sacred, because this is eternal. That a man may love God it is necessary that there should be not only a God to be loved, but a man to love him."[8] Again, God is God, and creatures are creatures. And ne'er the twain shall merge.

Second, we can rejoice in the plurality that characterizes the non-human creation. We aren't God. But neither are we snail darters or poodles or cows. God wants us to care for the other kinds of beings that he has placed in the world. This doesn't mean merging with them; it means accepting them for what they are.

One of the delightful things about the creation drama, as it is recounted in Genesis 1, is the delight that God takes in creating the manyness of the nonhuman kinds. Consider, for example, the creation of the sea creatures (Gen. 1:20–22). There is nothing grim or matter-of-fact about the way God does this. His tone is almost playful when he commands, "Let the waters bring forth swarms!" And when he actually sees the water teeming with all those sea creatures, he cries out in delight, "This is good!" Then he goes on to bless the swarms. God seems to enjoy a good "swarm."

And God wants us to enjoy the swarms, too. But to enjoy the non-human creatures doesn't mean making believe that they are human beings. Nor does it mean treating them as mere objects to manipulated by us for our own profit or pleasure. It means allowing them to be the "kinds" that God created them to be.

I once attended a meeting of Christian farmers in western Canada. They got together for an evening each month to talk about what it means to be Christians in their farming practices. The night I sat in on their discussion, they were talking about raising chickens. It was very impressive.

They were critical of the ways in which many of their fellow farmers raise chickens. Too often chickens get treated as if they were nothing but little egg-producing machines or little feathery bundles of white meat and dark meat. These Christian farmers thought it was wrong to squeeze chickens together in a dark cramped place with no room to move around. Chickens should be given an open space in which to parade in front of the other adult chickens, and to chase their young, and even to go off to their own private little corners to brood for a while.

These Christian farmers weren't romanticizing chickens. They weren't insisting that people should never eat eggs or that we should burn down all the fried chicken drive-ins. They know that chickens aren't people. But, as one of them said—and when he said it, it struck me as a very profound statement—"Chickens are chickens, after all, and they deserve to be *treated* like chickens!"

It is important to keep in mind that there are different kinds of things in the world. Having "dominion" over them (Gen. 1:28) doesn't mean dominating them. It means helping them to be the kinds of beings that God intends them to be.

Third, there is an intra-human plurality. Here too Chesterton makes the point well. The love that one person gives to another person is not a disguised form of self-love—as if the only way I can really love my wife is to see the two of us as actually being one self. When two people come to view themselves as a single "RiLeschardlie," an important element of loving has been lost. Thinking about the needs of the other is no longer appropriate. Forgiveness and self-sacrifice and going the second mile all become irrelevant to what holds us together.

The love that God intends us to show to each other is a loving relationship between partners, between separate human selves who are bonded together by covenant.

There have even been theologians who have insisted that this covenantal love is to be found within the deity itself. They have argued for what is often called a "social model" of the Trinity. God is not an undifferentiated self-loving One. God is a community of three Persons bound together by covenantal love. In loving each other as real and distinct human selves, then, we are sharing in an eternal interpersonal love that flows from the very heart of who God is.

Christian Divinization

Spiritualizing monists promise us that we can get beyond the "manyness" that characterizes our present experience of reality. But, like the secular humanists whom they are attempting to correct, they cannot deliver on their promise. The manyness is just there. It won't go away. Ever. But that can't be our final word to the spiritualizing monists. Their quest for Oneness is based on a distorted truth. We must not condemn the distortion without also understanding clearly the truth that they have in fact distorted.

The truth is that biblical religion also cares deeply about unity. It promises us that we can become more "together" persons. And it also tells us that we can be more at one with God than may seem possible to us in our present brokenness.

I noted earlier that the spiritualizing monists are eager to make divine the secular. And in particular they want human beings to move ahead in this process. We can become divine, they tell us.

Divinization is often a very explicit emphasis in the teachings of cults and new religions. Christian critics of these groups sometimes give the impression that the very idea of divinization is totally repugnant to Christians. But this is misleading. For one thing, the divinization theme has long been a favorite in the Eastern Orthodox churches.

A popular saying in the Eastern church illustrates the importance this notion has for them: "God became man so that man might become God." Eastern Orthodox Christians are also fond of supporting their teaching by pointing to the way in which Jesus himself seems to support the divinization idea when, in the tenth chapter of John's Gospel, he approvingly quotes Psalm 82:6: "You are gods."

A Greek theologian, Georgios I. Mantzaridis, has written a little book that provides a very clear exposition of the Orthodox understanding of divinization. When God united himself to human nature in the incarnate Christ, argues Mantzaridis, humanness was infused with a new measure of "divinizing grace," making it possible for each of us to be filled with the "uncreated divine energy."

But this does not mean that the boundaries between Creator and creature have thereby become blurred. This divinization teaching, Mantzaridis insists, does "not, of course, alter the basic distinction between man and God as created and Creator"; the doctrine is not meant to encourage "a pantheistic identification of man with God." Our divinization "is not realized through participation in God's essence but through communion in His divine energy. Man may share in God's glory and brightness, but the divine essence remains inaccessible and nonparticable. Thus the deified man is made god in all things, but he neither is identified with the divine essence nor shares in it."[9]

These are very instructive qualifying comments. We must not understand divinization as a process of coming to share in the very essence of God. God remains God. And we remain creatures—albeit "divinized" ones.

This Orthodox teaching is not meant, then, as a blurring of the metaphysical boundaries that separate the Creator from the creation. But isn't it nonetheless a dangerous way of talking about the way in which we are transformed by God's grace?

Well, in a sense it is. But it is also a legitimate attempt to take hold of a biblical theme that cannot be ignored. We pointed to this theme earlier. When the serpent tells Eve that she can be "like God," he is, we said, trading on a significant subtlety. She *was* created to be "like God"—she was fashioned in the very image of her divine Maker.

We mustn't allow the fact of the serpent's distortion to hide the important truth here. It might be that the best way of countering the false promise of divinization, as it is offered by today's spiritualizing monists, is to follow the lead of the Eastern Orthodox—by pointing to the wonderful and mysterious sense in which we can become "divinized" without becoming God!

Longing for Change

I was once asked to give the opening and closing addresses at a Christian organization's annual convention. Their topic that year was change, and my talks were to deal with an overall biblical perspective on the fact of change. How should Christians view change? Is it bad as such? How do we cope with the shock of the new?

I began my preparations with a very simple exercise. I took my Bible concordance off the shelf and looked up all the variations of the word *change*. Nothing really captured my imagination until I got to the reference in 1 Corinthians 15:51–52: "Lo! I tell you a mystery. We shall not all sleep, but we shall all be changed, in a moment, in the twinkling of an eye, at the last trumpet. For the trumpet will sound, and the dead will be raised imperishable, and we shall be changed." Immediately I went to the tape player and listened to Handel's great rendition of this passage in the *Messiah*. And for the next several days, as I worked on my speeches, I played that tape over and over.

"Lo! I tell you a mystery . . . we shall be changed!" Not only do Christians not oppose change as such, we ought to yearn for the kind of change God has promised us.

"It does not yet appear what we shall be, but we know that when he appears we shall be like him, for we shall see him as he is" (1 John 3:3) — not we shall *be* him, but we shall be *like* him. That in itself, though, is no small matter. "We shall be changed."

My favorite C. S. Lewis piece is his essay "The Weight of Glory." Someday, Lewis tells us, we who are in Christ will "shine as the sun, we are to be given the Morning Star." Of course, Lewis notes, it may not be a good thing for a Christian "to think too much of his potential glory hereafter." But, he immediately adds,

it is hardly possible for him to think too often or too deeply about that of his neighbour. The load, or weight, or burden of my neighbour's glory should be laid daily on my back, a load so heavy that only humility can carry it, and the backs of the proud will be broken. It is a serious thing to live in a society of possible gods and goddesses, to remember that the dullest and most interesting person you talk to may one day be a creature which, if you saw it now, you would be strongly tempted to worship, or else a horror and a corruption such as you now meet, if at all, only in a nightmare. All day long we are, in some degree, helping each other to one or other of these destinations.[10]

There are two very important points that Lewis is making here about divinization. One is that the promise of becoming God-like shouldn't function as an excuse for self-indulgence; it should inspire us to think about how we might affect the lives of others, as they move toward their future.

The other is that there is no guarantee that all human beings are moving toward glorification. We are not all on an inevitable evolutionary climb toward perfect harmony.

The "RiLeschardlie" team tells us that at one point in their allegorical journey they met Attila the Hun. They find this cruel murderer very repulsive. But soon they discover that Attila isn't an independently existing phenomenon—"Attila's a part of me, too, part of everyone who ever held a murderous thought." The villainous butchers of history are a part of "the disguise that is evil." They are the negative possibilities that we must overcome if we are to achieve cosmic harmony. We can banish this evil "disguise" if we immerse ourselves in the reality of love.

Spiritualizing monism has difficulty accounting for the reality of evil. Everything that is real must be a part of the harmonious One. What we think of as evil, then, is either an illusion or it is a disguised good, a necessary step in the movement of Love.

The Bible does not allow us to accept this portrayal of the way things are. Evil is very real. We human beings cannot just "love" it away. We can only long for the time when injustice and oppression will be banished from the new creation. We can act in the here and now with the assurance that that will happen, but we cannot make it happen. It will be God's doing. "And we shall be changed."

Jesus the Unifier

When I was growing up in the conservative-evangelical world, I heard many attacks on "oneness." One such attack stands out in my memory. It was a sermon by a well-known conservative preacher in which he warned us against getting worked up over "unity." The promise of unity is a trick of the Devil. Indeed, the preacher said, Satan has a three-pronged campaign for unity that he is promoting in our day: one world race, one world church, and one world government. True Christians, that preacher insisted, will oppose, then, the civil rights movement, the World Council of Churches, and the United Nations.

I don't think he used this line, but he might as well have: "What God has put asunder, let no human being join together."

That kind of thinking had an influence on me in my youth. Later on, I gradually moved away from that sort of "separatistic" mentality. But it wasn't until a few years ago that I saw in a very direct way what was wrong with that preacher's sermon.

I was reading in Saint Peter's first epistle, and suddenly these words leaped out at me: "But you are a chosen race, a royal priesthood, a holy nation" (1 Pet. 2:9).

This was one of those "Aha!" experiences. I realized that the apostle was addressing the same agenda that was dealt with in that preacher's sermon. And Peter was insisting that Jesus has put together a new kind of race, a new kind of religious community, and a new kind of nation.

The same topic is treated in the Book of Revelation, where the Apostle John witnesses the heavenly throng singing a "new song" to the Lamb:

Worthy art thou to take the scroll and to open its seals,
for thou wast slain and by thy blood didst ransom men and women
    for God
from every tribe and tongue and people and nation,
and hast made them a kingdom and priests to our God,
and they shall reign on earth.

(Rev. 5:9-10)

Jesus is in the business of promoting unity. He is making something new happen in human communities—reaching into our present racial and religious and national brokenness and *making* "a kingdom and priests to our God."

The preacher was wrong in his insistence that only the Devil cares about oneness. Jesus isn't in favor of our present patterns of brokenness and separation, our clannishness and our party rivalries. God sent Jesus into the world to fulfill the ancient prophecy: "You shall be called the repairer of the breach" (Isa. 58:12).

This means that Christians can't be against unity as such. If we oppose a specific attempt at oneness, it will have to be on the grounds that it is promoting the wrong kind of unity.

My preacher deserves partial credit on this point. He was right to ask whether the unity at which various movements aim is of the satanic variety. The Devil is a counterfeiter. And there should be no doubt in our minds – he will not adopt a hands-off attitude toward such prominent programs as the civil rights movement, the ecumenical quest, and the attempt to promote closer cooperation among the nations. We would do well to keep an eye out for indications of distorted unity in these efforts. But we can also celebrate the ways in which they provide us with signs of the kind of oneness that Jesus desires.

It may seem like a long way from the examples of unity I have mentioned here to the spiritualizing monists quest for cosmic harmony, but it really isn't. The desire to merge with the One doesn't just strike people out of the blue. Oneness is attractive to them because they have come to have problems with manyness. And the frustrations with manyness that get them going on the monistic quest are often very mundane matters: difficulties in getting along with other people, a sense that their lives have become fractured into pieces that are difficult to put back together again, the gnawing conviction that there are just too many different value systems, too many religions, too many ideologies and political prescriptions, too many cultures – too much manyness.

For people like that, the promise of oneness sounds like good news.

The Christian good news also addresses these frustrations, these hopes and fears about oneness and manyness. What the gospel promises is not the unity that comes with undifferentiated Being – it doesn't encourage us to hope that all differences will be wiped out – what the Bible teaches is that unity comes from having the right kind of relationship with Jesus. He gives us oneness without destroying plurality.

When we come to know Jesus, the manyness doesn't vanish. But we see it all in a different light:

For in him all things were created, in heaven and on earth, visible and invisible, whether thrones or dominions or principalities or authorities—all things were created through him and for him. He is before all things, and in him all things hold together.

(Col. 1:15–16)

That's good news for people who are tempted by the monistic impulse!

6. Reenchanting Reality

On a speaking trip to the midwest a few years ago, I was asked what I thought about Mafu. My questioner must have thought I had a special line on Mafu, since I live rather near to where he had been hovering.

Mafu is a spirit guide who once walked the earth as a leper in ancient Pompeii. In recent years Mafu is reported to have been speaking his mind on a regular basis, with the cooperation of Penny Torres, a Southern California housewife who has "channeled" him during meetings in her living room. A number of people, including some well-known television personages, have paid large fees for the opportunity to listen to Ms. Torres speak Mafu's words.

So, because I was a philosopher from Southern California visiting the midwest during the time that Penny Torres's channeling had been in the news, my questioner asked me, "What do you think of Mafu?"

My instinct was to offer a light-hearted answer: "Mafu seems quite a harmless fellow; actually, he sounds like a lot of other people who hang around Santa Monica!"

But my questioner would have nothing of that. "No, what do you *really* think? As a *Christian* ? Is Penny Torres pulling our leg? Is she deluded? Or demon-possessed? Or is this more like the witch of Endor case?"

I immediately picked up on this reference to Saul's visit to Endor, a story recorded in 1 Samuel 28.

I told my questioner that I'm not quite sure what it means to say that Penny Torres's channeling is "more like the witch of Endor case." That's because I'm not very clear about what really went on at Endor. Did Saul actually encounter the spirit of

Samuel? Did the witch conjure up a vision of Samuel? Was the witch pulling Saul's leg? Were both Saul and the witch deluded? Was this a case of demonic activity?

I don't know. I do get the impression from the biblical account that something supernatural occurred at Endor. There even seems to be a strong suggestion that Saul actually communicated with the departed Samuel: "And Saul knew that it was Samuel. . . . Then Samuel said to Saul . . ." (1 Samuel 28: 14–15). The language here – "knew," "said" – doesn't seem to hedge much, but I still wouldn't stake my reputation on a specific interpretation of the metaphysics of the story.

Looking for Biblical Answers

I do not mean to promote skepticism about biblical teaching on topics of this sort, but I do think that it is important to be clear about the *kind* of teaching the Bible offers us in our attempts to understand such phenomena. And, frankly, I don't find the Bible giving us much help in our efforts to understand the precise details of what was going on in Penny Torres's channeling sessions.

I'm not pleased about my inability to give a clearer answer than that. I am very curious about these topics, and I don't think my curiosity is particularly unhealthy. As a philosopher I am interested in metaphysical questions; that is, questions about what is or is not "real." And the question of what is "really" going on in the Mafu case strikes me as a legitimate application of that metaphysical interest.

Moreover, as a *Christian* philosopher I sense an obligation to give intellectual guidance to my fellow believers about how they are to view the world in a Christian manner. This means (as I understand the way Christians ought to think about philosophical issues) that we must allow our worldview to be shaped by the way the Bible portrays reality. And on the face of things, at least, it seems to me very proper to go to the Bible with the question, What are we to think of Mafu? So I do find it frustrating not to be able to find a clear answer.

That doesn't mean, though, that I think God is somehow cheating us by not giving us biblical answers to our questions about the metaphysics of Mafu. There are many good questions that we bring to the Bible that are not answered in a direct way. That doesn't make the questions any less good, nor the Bible any less authoritative. The Bible simply doesn't answer all of our good questions.

When the Bible leaves legitimate and important questions unanswered, we must assume it is for our good – even though that may require some trust on our part. Consider, for example, questions that arise in medical decision making. A little baby is permanently brain-damaged, kept alive only by advanced life-support machines. The child will never laugh or crawl or push away a bottle. But for all of that, the child is recognizably a living human being. Should we subject the parents to years of hospital vigils and astronomical medical expenses? Or should we disconnect the machinery and allow the baby to die?

These are important questions, agonizing questions. But the Bible doesn't answer them in any direct or obvious way. I wish it did. In cases like this I yearn for explicit and detailed guidance from God. But the Bible doesn't give it.

To say that the Bible doesn't give the answers, though, doesn't mean that *God* doesn't give them. The Bible isn't the only place where God provides us with the truth.

Jesus promised that "when the Spirit of truth comes, he will guide you into all the truth" (John 16:13). And the Holy Spirit accomplishes this "guiding" in more ways than simply by pointing us to specific Bible passages. The Spirit supports us and leads us as we struggle with very difficult challenges in ways that draw upon biblical guidelines and sensitivities. The hard-earned, and sometimes very partial, answers that we get when we agonize over complicated questions must also be viewed as guidance from God.

Actually, this seems to be the very point of the Bible's silence regarding the detailed ethical guidance that we long for in difficult situations. God wants us to develop moral maturity, to learn to exercise discernment. The agony of decision making is good for us.

And the same holds for many questions about the metaphysical makeup of the spirit world. Recognizing that the Bible does not provide us with detailed accounts of this area of reality, we can still work with what we do have, in the hope of struggling with the issues in a faithful, biblically sensitive manner. To do this is a means of Christian growth.

We will soon take a look at the sense in which it *is* possible for us to gain a biblically faithful perspective on the metaphysics of Mafu. But first we have to understand more clearly why occultism is an important topic for Christians to struggle with.

An Occult 'Revival'?

B. F. Skinner is a well-known behaviorist psychologist. As a behaviorist, Skinner is convinced that the time has come to do away with the notion of an "inner" life. We human persons are purely physical beings who engage in overt behaviors in response to environmental stimuli. As Skinner views things, positing "invisible" ideas or purposes to explain why people behave the way they do simply has no function. The suggestion that minds are real is a useless hypothesis; it explains nothing.

Skinner's best-known defense of his perspective is his *Beyond Freedom and Dignity.* In that book he cites a historical precedent for his own proposal that we get rid of the idea of a mind. Look at what has happened to the belief in demon-possession, Skinner says. There was a time when it was thought that you could not explain certain human behaviors without believing in demons. But this way of viewing things is no longer acceptable. We now know better. Today we all see that the idea of demon-possession is a useless hypothesis. Skinner is aware, of course, that there are still people around who believe in demons. He explicitly acknowledges that this is so. But those folks are not to be taken seriously. He minces no words on this point: "Intelligent people no longer believe that men are possessed by demons."[1] And it is about time that we decide the same thing about the notion of a mind.

Skinner published his book in 1971, and I have the clear sense that today his comments about demon-possession lack the force that they had when he first published them. I've often wondered, for example, what B. F. Skinner would say about the fact that only a few years after he wrote his book, the novel *The Exorcist* became a best-seller, and people were soon lining up for blocks to see the movie version of that fictional portrayal of contemporary demon-possession.

And *The Exorcist* was no isolated phenomenon in the 1970s and 1980s. Occult beliefs and practices became "hot" topics, both intellectually and commercially. Some university psychologists announced that the techniques of Peruvian shamans have more therapeutic value than the methods those professors had been advocating in their own textbooks. And there were English professors who joined witches' covens. Tarot cards, astrology charts, crystals, "pyramid power" handbooks—all of these became highly marketable merchandise. And Penny Torres started to channel Mafu.

Obviously, not all of these items can be evaluated in exactly the same way. *The Exorcist*, for example, was no celebration of pagan thought and practice. If anything, it encouraged us to view the ancient Christian rite of exorcism as still very relevant to contemporary life. But even so, the novel and movie fit a larger mood of fascination with spirits and magical rituals and the "paranormal."

This fascination became so widespread that commentators have taken to describing the 1970s and 1980s as a time when Western culture witnessed an "occult revival" or an "occult explosion."

There does seem to be something fitting about that characterization. Think again of the B. F. Skinner example. In 1971 he could get away with claiming that intelligent people just don't take the idea of the demonic seriously anymore. The people who edited his book, and the scholars who wrote the early reviews of it, probably read that line without even pausing to wonder about it. But a decade later it would have raised some eyebrows. Fascination with demons in civilized circles was by that time something that could not be ignored.

When I was in graduate school, I had long arguments with a fellow student who was very anti-Christian. His own perspective was a rather straightforward secular humanism; he had no use for any kind of religious perspective. I was a source of puzzlement to him. He could not get over the fact that I was an evangelical Christian. After all, he liked to tell me, in other ways I seemed to be pretty intelligent!

A decade after those conversations I ran into him at a scholarly convention. "I've become religious," he announced almost immediately. When I inquired into the nature of his conversion he told me that he was now "into Navajo religion." His new perspective had given him "a whole new way of relating to the universe." When he found out that I was still an evangelical Christian, he gave me the same bemused look that he had so often during our student days, but this time his bemusement came at me from a different direction. "I just don't see how you can buy into something that's so *tame!*" he said.

My friend was caught up in a new fascination with the occult. But was he part of an occult "revival"?

Some scholars who study the history of the occult don't like this way of describing what has been happening in recent decades. Their dissatisfaction is spelled out clearly in a fascinating essay, "Explaining Modern Occultism," by Robert Galbreath. To describe something as a "revival," Galbreath observes, "denotes a revitalization or renewal of something that is (or is perceived as) dormant, decadent, dead, or otherwise deficient." When we speak of an "occult revival," then, we are "presupposing a preceding period in which the occult was moribund, minor, or even nonexistent."[2]

But it is difficult to find such a period in American life, Galbreath argues. He offers an analogy: political activity doesn't disappear between elections; it just doesn't receive the focused attention that it does during times of campaigning. And the same holds for occult practice. Occultism has been there all along in

North American popular culture. What has been happening lately is that the occult has been getting more public attention. It has been discovered by the educated elites.

Re-enchantment

The occult, then, hasn't been "revived." It has been there all along, but it has become a more visible phenomenon in recent years.

But what *is* this pattern that has begun to spark the interest of so many people, including those "intelligent people" whom B. F. Skinner thought had long given up on this sort of thing?

"Occult" comes from a Latin word that means "hidden" or "concealed." Occultism often emphasizes the existence and importance of beings that are concealed from the ordinary view. Demons and ascended masters fall outside the definitions of reality espoused by common sense, scientific study, or official church teachings. Occultists also claim to possess extraordinary techniques for getting things accomplished—spells, incantations, healing rites—that are known only by tapping into a fund of wisdom that has long been the secret property of an in-group.

Obviously, occult teachings and practices do not fit well into the universe as it has been defined by secular humanism. As the great German sociologist Max Weber said in his well-known essay on the modern scientific outlook, we moderns live in a world that has been "disenchanted": the universe has been emptied of "mysterious powers," and now we believe that we "can, in principle, master all things by calculation."[3]

For many intellectuals, the arrival of this "disenchanted" perspective on reality is a welcome and irreversible accomplishment of civilized humanity. It is not surprising, then, that a B. F. Skinner could state without embarrassment in 1971 that "intelligent people" simply don't entertain the possibility of demon-possession anymore.

Galbreath's comments regarding the persistence of occult beliefs and practices tells us, though, that the educated elites have not done a very effective job of communicating the requirements of "civilization" to the general populace. And now it is becoming clear that they haven't even been able to convince themselves.

Like monism, occultism is a signal that there are intelligent folks around who are uneasy with the picture of reality conveyed by secular humanism. We might say that the newer occultism is a signal of discontent with the accepted version of what it means to be "modern." The occultists are attempting to "reenchant" the world.

Figuring Out the Occult

Actually, there are two different signals being sent by means of the recent widespread interest in the occult, one negative and the other positive.

The negative message is a no to the secular humanists. Peter Berger once observed that it would be wrong-headed to assume that the young members of satanist cults are primarily motivated by discontent with the religious teachings of the established churches. Rather, he argued, they are thumbing their noses at the teachers who taught them a thoroughgoing secularism in their university classrooms.[4]

Berger's point is well taken. As stated, though, it portrays the occult phenomenon mainly as a negative gesture. And in some cases involvement in the occult may not be anything more than that. It might well be, for example, that some young folks join satanist cults, not because they believe in Satan, but because they want to do something that will shock their secular humanist elders.

(Some people might decide to live their lives *only* as a negative gesture. This is a way of acting out the nihilism that we will look at in the next chapter.)

The positive signal is the effort to reenchant the universe. For many people, occultism is in itself an attractive way of viewing reality. It is important for Christians for figure out why people specifically choose occultism as their positive alternative to secular humanism. After all, there are other possibilities. A disillusioned secular humanist could become a spiritualizing monist—or a Christian.

Why, then, is the occult option so attractive to many of our contemporaries? Why the widespread effort these days to reenchant the universe?

This brings us back to the question of how the Bible can help us understand the metaphysics of Mafu. The Bible, we said, doesn't give us detailed guidance in mapping out the details of the occult world. In what sense, then, does it help us to figure on what is "going on" in occult beliefs and practices?

I must make it clear that I am not implying that the Bible says nothing at all about the nature of the spirit world. At the very least, the Bible tells us that there *is* a realm of unseen spiritual realities. It tells us about a God who can only be properly worshiped in spirit and in truth. And it tells us about angels and a personal Devil.

We can acknowledge the reality of the spirit world, however, yet still not know how to assess specific occult beliefs and practices. In the same way, we can trust a guidebook that tells us there are great antique bargains to be found in London yet still not know where exactly the bargains are to be found or how to tell a phony from the genuine article.

One night when I was a college student, I experimented with a Ouija board. We were having a party. Someone produced the board, and a group of us had a go at it. We really did get some "messages" that seemed to be directed toward specific participants. It was an eerie experience, and I could tell that the others were as nervous as I was. Finally one person said, "I don't think we should be messing with this sort of thing." We all agreed. And for me at least, that was my first and last occult experiment.

I still don't have a strong theory about what was going on—metaphysically speaking—in that episode. Maybe one of my friends was consciously controlling the process. Maybe we were all unconsciously working to create the "messages." Maybe it was all happenstance. Maybe some supernatural power was communicating with us. Or maybe it was a combination of two or more of these factors.

I don't know. Furthermore, I'm not even sure how I could decide for sure—or what would count as a decisive explanation. I certainly don't see any *biblical* basis for preferring one explanation over another.

But neither is the Bible's message irrelevant to this topic. The Bible may not provide me with detailed metaphysical information, but it certainly shapes the perspective that I bring to my search for explanations of that sort of thing.

The Epistle to the Colossians is instructive in this regard. The apostle was writing to Christians who lived in a cultural setting in which much was made of "elemental spirits." The citizens of Colossae believed that there were spirits who controlled various aspects of reality. If you wanted to be successful in a given area— business, sports, romance, child-bearing, politics—you had to ingratiate yourself with the spirits that specialized in that kind of activity.

Paul makes it very clear that Christians are not to be involved in these attempts to placate the spirit world: "See to it that no one makes a prey of you by philosophy and empty deceit, according to human tradition, according to the elemental spirits of the universe, and not according to Christ" (Col. 2:8). And again, a little further on: "If with Christ you died to the elemental spirits of the universe, why do you live as if you still belonged to the world?" (Col. 3:20).

Now here is an obvious question: when the apostle tells Christians not to think "according to the elemental spirits of the universe," is he implying that these spirits do exist but that we are not to bother with them? Or is he saying that we should stop believing that beings of that sort actually do exist?

It's not easy to tell for sure. But to dwell on these questions is to miss the point of what Paul *is* clearly saying. There can be no mistaking that he is telling us not to follow the way of life associated with a belief in the reality of elemental spirits. Nothing that exists can rival the supreme Lordship of Jesus Christ. Whether there are such spirits or not, then, we are to live as disciples of Jesus.

The Bible typically deals with these issues in the way a mother might address the fears of her child. The child says, "I can't go to sleep, because I'm afraid the goblins will get me!"

"Don't be afraid," the mother replies. "Mommy is right here, and I won't let anything hurt you."

The mother doesn't speak directly to the metaphysics of the situation. There is no telling, from what the mother has actually said, whether or not she shares the child's belief that goblins are real. In an important sense, though, she does speak to that belief. She reassures the child that there is no need to be afraid of any goblins that might exist.

Similarly, the Bible makes it very clear to us that nothing in the spirit world—however that world might actually be populated—can rival God's authority and power. That is the clear message of the Endor story. We may not be able to spell out the metaphysical geography of Endor on the basis of what the biblical narrative tells us, but whatever the exact character of the witch's exercise of her craft—whether it be a case of trickery, self-deception, or cooperation with supernatural forces—there can be no mistaking that Saul's trip to Endor was a refusal to trust in God's wisdom.

The Occult Impulse as Unique

The Bible doesn't offer a detailed map of the occult world. We might say that the biblical writers are more interested in spiritual psychology than they are in spiritual geography.

I'm not using "psychology" here in a technical sense. The Bible isn't a textbook in personality theory or child development. Nor do I mean to give a reductionistic account of the biblical message—as if the Bible is only concerned with our psychological lives, narrowly construed.

But the Scriptures do give special attention to our fundamental motivations, to the basic meanings that we attribute to things. And that's the way in which the biblical writers typically deal with the question of what is "going on" in occult beliefs and practices.

This is why I made such a big point in an earlier chapter about the centrality of trust in a Christian view of human nature. Our trustings are what give basic direction to our lives. They are the primary steering mechanisms of our human journeys.

Because our trustings are so important, they need to be probed carefully. It is not adequate, for example, simply to say that people either trust God or they trust something else. That's true, but it is not enough. It is also necessary to probe the specific character of our trustings. For one thing, we Christians need to be clear that we are trusting God for the right reasons. And we also need to be sensitive to the reasons why other people – people who do not trust God – choose the specific patterns of trusting that will give direction to their lives.

Occultism is a unique way of trusting. We will miss something of its meaning if we simply subsume it under some larger heading. That's why I am deliberately treating occultism as a pattern that is distinguishable from monism.

Many Christian commentators on contemporary "isms" lump monism and occultism together as components of the New Age movement. But that is misleading. For one thing, we can't rightly understand either of these "isms" by simply seeing them as parts of the New Age – a movement that may well be a passing fad.

But it is not even helpful to link them closely in our analyses of New Age thinking. Douglas Groothuis gets at this concern nicely when he observes that the New Age movement itself actually falls into two distinct categories: "mainstream New Age and occult New Age."[5] The New Age movement has put its blessing on occult beliefs and practices, but this blessing means different things to different New Age groups.

The "mainstream" New Agers – the spiritualizing monists – make much, as we have seen, of the need to overcome long-standing polarities. Monists look favorably upon occult beliefs and practices because the occult phenomenon is one important example of how modern people are searching for a new consciousness in which, for example, the old opposition between science and magic is transcended. But from the monist perspective, this is at best a stage along the way. Ultimately it is not the acceptance of magic that is important, but the overcoming of polarities as we move toward merger with the One.

There are other people, though, who appreciate the occult for its own sake. Involvement in occultism isn't for them just a symbol of a new emerging consciousness; they consider the occult view of reality to be the right way to understand the universe.

Groothuis is correct in insisting that there are two different New Age perspectives on the occult. But my concern here is not primarily with clarifying what should be included within the New Age movement. The New Age as an identifiable phenomenon may not last very long, but monistic and occultist impulses will not pass from the scene very quickly. And it is important to understand the differences between these unique impulses.

It is a good thing to pay attention to the differences among spiritual psychologies. The dynamics at work in one person's desire to merge with the One can be very different from those that operate in another person's fascination with occult powers.

It is certainly important to pay attention to these differences for evangelistic purposes. Let me draw a simple analogy. You can't witness to the power of the gospel in exactly the same way on a street corner in skid row and at a convention of stockbrokers. Of course, the unbelieving derelicts and the unbelieving stockbrokers do have one thing in common. They are unbelievers, which means they are not trusting in God. They are organizing their lives around a commitment to something creaturely rather than to the Creator.

That certainly is a common bond between them. Both groups are engaged in idolatry. But it is no insignificant fact that they have chosen different idols. The derelict has most likely organized his or her life around booze—let goods and kindred go, this mortal life also, just let me drink!—whereas the stockbroker has more likely chosen an idolatrous attachment to money or power or prestige.

The answer for each of them is to form a trusting relationship with God. But we must also pay attention to what each must *let go of* in order effectively to reach out to God. Letting go of booze in order to take hold of God's promises is different from letting go of financial power in order to take hold of those same promises.

In a similar way, the spiritual psychology of monism is different from that of occultism. Turning away from the quest to merge with the One is not the same as turning away from efforts to control reality by means of spells and charms and magical rites. That's why it is important to look at the uniqueness of the occultist project.

Unique Dangers

I want to try to put the best face that I can on some key features of the occultists' way of viewing reality. But first I need to make it clear that I am aware that these are not issues to be treated lightly.

The occult network is in many ways a very dangerous phenomenon. In the area where I live and work, for example, there is growing concern in the counseling and law enforcement communities about the evidence that many cases of child abuse are linked to occult practices.

There is much about occultism that is frightening—frightening, but not surprising. In Romans 1, the apostle describes various ways in which people can be "given over" to evil passions and projects. And the possibility that we can become "possessed" by the evil that we flirt with is never greater than when we engage in open and brazen attempts to enter into league with the very powers of evil.

My earlier comments about our not having maps of the geography of the spirit world might strike some people as needlessly agnostic. I make no apologies for them, though. In a literal sense, to be an agnostic about a given topic is to say "I don't know" about that subject matter. On the details of occult reality, I am an agnostic.

When I hear some Christian leaders talk with great authority about, say, the numbers and names and habits of demons, I get nervous. Much of what they say strikes me as fantasy.

But I am *not* agnostic about the reality of the Evil One. I can't fill in the details of what was going on at Endor, but I have no doubt that Satan was at work there.

When I try to think of plausible reasons why people are attracted to occultism, then, I do not mean to ignore the reality of satanic influence. Indeed, to think about the attractiveness of the occult perspective is to take that influence very seriously. The Devil is subtle. He distorts important truths, which means that he often gets at us by working on very significant human hopes and fears.

The Attractions of the Occult

Let's look, then, at some of the attractive features of occultism. I will focus on four of them.

Occultism is an attempt to recover a sense of mystery. I have already credited spiritualizing monism with an interest in restoring mystery. But that interest is both more intense and of a different sort among the occultists.

A while back, the child psychologist Bruno Bettleheim wrote a book in which he makes a strong case for the importance of fairy tales in bringing up children. These stories, he says, deal with "the eternal questions," such as, "What is the world really like? How am I to live my life in it? How can I truly be myself?" The fairy tale addresses these topics, not in abstract philosophical terms, but in a way that leaves it "to the child's fantasizing whether and how to apply to himself what the story reveals about life and human nature."[6]

In other words, fairy stories free us to fantasize about the basic issues of life. And this is healthy, argues Bettleheim. It is good for us to be presented with situations and images and characters that get our imagination working. It is also good for us to be drawn into stories that evoke experiences of sadness and surprise and delight as we encounter basic human realities. As J.R.R. Tolkien once said, a good fairy story is one that never fails to make us catch our breath and feel relief when the happy ending comes, no matter how many times we have heard the story.

Bettleheim thinks that contemporary youth often engage in deviant behavior because they were deprived of the magic of fairy stories in their childhood:

It is as if these young people feel that now is their last chance to make up for a severe deficiency in their life experience; or that without having had a period of belief in magic, they will be unable to meet the rigors of adult life. Many young people who today suddenly seek escape in drug-induced dreams, apprentice themselves to some guru, believe in astrology, engage in practicing "black magic," or who in some other fashion escape from reality into daydreams about magic experiences which are to change their life for the better, were prematurely pressed to view reality in an adult way. Trying to evade reality in such ways has its deeper cause in early formative experiences which prevented the development of the conviction that life can be mastered in realistic ways.[7]

I like Bettleheim's book very much. It is a rich resource for understanding the value of myth and fantasy. But in spite of his strong defense of fairy stories, I do find him a bit condescending toward the values that they embody.

Consider the passage I just quoted. It's obvious that Bettleheim thinks that a sense of "magic" is tied to a stage that we must all go through if we are to be healthy people. Since young people today are often deprived of this stage, they aren't capable of moving on to a "realistic" mastery of life's problems.

And Bettleheim does think we must all move on from the magic stage. He is convinced that a healthy individual development will go through the same stages that the human race as a whole has gone through. And since the human race once went through a primitive "mythical" phase, each of us as individuals must also go through a time when we feel the "magic." But it is something we outgrow.

I don't agree. We never really outgrow the need for the sense of mystery and magic that Bettleheim rightly sees as so important to the world of fairy stories. This is not to say, however, that we should never pass beyond the child's understanding of reality; what we need is an *adult* sense of mystery and magic. And this is what secular humanism has deprived us all of in its "civilizing" project. It is no wonder that contemporary people are unhappy living in a world that has been "disenchanted."

Occultism wants to re-personalize reality. A world that has come to be wholly dominated by science and technology is a lonely and frightening place in which to live. Here is how Helmut Thielicke has described the spiritual dynamics of living in that kind of world:

Those who no longer fear God fear everything in the world. For when the Father is not there this world becomes something that is utterly incalculable. When it has become a great repository of the incalculable, loaded with explosive and immeasurable possibilities, it begins to radiate fear and anxiety: fear of the monster contingency. Then it triggers in man a kind of counterreaction in which he resorts to magical formulas with which he seeks to ward off the threat. Thus in the very midst of the cool, objective precincts of this post-rationalist world, in the very structures made of glass and concrete, the architectonic symbols of objectivity, there flickers the murky light of superstition and all its rank tropical growths.[8]

It is interesting to compare Thielicke's description here with Max Weber's account of "disenchantment," which I referred to earlier. Weber tells us that by getting rid of the "mysterious powers" that had previously populated the universe, we scientifically oriented folks can now "master all things by calculation." But Thielicke argues that this is precisely what secular humanism makes it impossible for us to do: when we depersonalize the universe by getting rid of a loving God, the world "becomes something that is utterly incalculable."

Secular humanism fails to accomplish the very thing it sets out to do. By attempting to bring reality under the control of human science and technology, it actually makes the world less familiar and less manageable. A depersonalized universe is a stark and lonely place to live.

The occultists know this. And so they attempt to bring the "mysterious powers" back. Spirits may not be always very easy to analyze and control, but at least they fill our world with signals of purpose and meaning. After all, our human friends aren't always very predictable either, but it is nice to have them around. When you have an overwhelming desire to feel at home in the world, predictability isn't everything!

Occultism is a search for a story. Channeling is easy to ridicule. It is difficult for many of us to take Mafu seriously. But if we probe a little, the channeling phenomenon starts to look a little less silly.

Not only have modern people lost the feeling that the universe is a familiar place; they are often not even very familiar with each other. This is certainly the case in those locales where channeling seems to be most common.

Channeling often appeals to the uprooted. We might even say that it appeals to the *un*rooted, to people who have no extended families, no sense of tradition, no feeling that they are *from* some place.

This has long been the experience of many black Americans. The slave traders tore them away from their home countries, and slave owners broke up their families. Their collective cultural memory grew dim. This is why the "roots" phenomenon—of which Alex Haley's book by that name was a highly visible sign—was so important. For many Afro-Americans it meant discovering their collective story.

For many of our contemporaries, however, there is no story to discover. They are genuinely unrooted.

Channeling speaks to this problem. It gives people an instant story. After you have spent an hour with Mafu, you have forged some links to the past. You and the other folks at the seance now have a friend in ancient Babylon. You can begin to see how your life might actually fit into a larger narrative. You have been "connecting." You have discovered a new kind of "networking."

Occultism is a quest for authoritative guidance. It is no accident that Mafu and his like are referred to as "spirit *guides*" and "ascended *masters*." The people who attend channeling sessions want to know how to live their lives. Their culture is pervaded with conflicting claims on their loyalty, and they are confused. Occult practice puts them in touch with a spiritual expertise that is a cut above the ordinary flux of human opinion, but it isn't so lofty that it seems far removed from their day-to-day concerns.

I'm not an expert in the sociology of religion, but I do devote quite a bit of my spare time to reading about cults and new religions. I'm especially interested in those movements that had their beginnings in nineteenth-century North America: Shakers, Mormons, Christian Scientists, and the like. I have been impressed by the fact that many of these groups got started because of a dissatisfaction with the "high God" of Calvinism.

I am a dyed-in-the-wool Calvinist, so that sort of dissatisfaction does not elicit automatic sympathy from me. But I can feel something of the dissatisfaction expressed by an Ann Lee or a Joseph Smith or a Mary Baker Eddy. The God of Calvinist orthodoxy—and of Lutheran and Roman Catholic and Anglican orthodoxies, to name a few others—has often been portrayed as a distant Father who has very little empathy for the daily hopes and fears of his children.

Many cults and new religions have attempted, then, to bring the spirit world a little closer to us mortals. They recognize that people need a sense of transcendence—but not so much transcendence that the divine realm becomes far removed from our existential situation.

The occultists have attacked this problem with a vengeance. Mafu and his fellow ascended masters are no mere mortals—they live at a different level of reality than the rest of us. But neither are they very far removed from the hopes and fears that are real to us. They represent a friendly transcendence, hovering near our cities and suburbs and towns, always willing to come right into our living rooms and offer us practical advice for living our lives in the twentieth century, very neighborly "masters" and "guides"!

Finding the Magic in the Gospel

Occultism speaks to legitimate hopes and fears people feel. The four features I just touched upon really are attractive. The occult way of addressing these legitimate human concerns is, however, a distortion of the truth. Christians have an important and exciting challenge: to untwist that which occultism has twisted.

I'm not going to try to do that here, though, by giving a point-by-point response to each of the four. For one thing, I have already given some indications in this chapter about how Christians might address them.

But I am also a bit nervous about point-by-point responses to issues raised by non-Christian groups. Evangelical apologists seem especially fond of working in that mode. They often provide charts and checklists that help us to see the superiority of Christianity over its contemporary rivals. These graphics encourage a scorecard mentality in dealing with alternative religious movements: evangelical Christianity gets 100 percent; Jehovah's Witnesses get 60 percent; Mormons 30 percent; satanists zero.

I'm not saying that the charts are completely unhelpful. But I do think that something is lost when we give the impression that we can arrive at a verdict by making point-by-point evaluations.

I don't want to be misunderstood. I can add up scores as well as the next apologist. And I am firmly convinced that occultism fails the test at every point. It locates the mystery in the wrong place; its personalization of reality is riddled with confusion; the story that it formulates is a fiction; and its "guides" and "masters" are charlatans.

But it isn't enough to say all that.

The brief account that I have given of four features of the occultist quest is, I think, a fair representation of why many people are drawn to occult beliefs and practices. To be sure, there is much more that can be said. But I am convinced that I have outlined some of occultism's genuine points of attraction.

I have made much of the fact that contemporary occultism draws a lot of its energy from a dissatisfaction with a naturalistic worldview. I sympathize with that dissatisfaction. And I believe with all my heart that only the gospel of Jesus Christ provides us with a satisfying alternative to naturalism.

But I can see why many of my contemporaries don't consider Christianity very satisfying. We proponents of traditional Christian thought haven't always done a very good job of presenting the gospel as an exciting alternative to naturalism. We may have better answers than the occultists do to the four points I have outlined, but we haven't always made that obvious.

I heard a Christian leader attack C. S. Lewis's writings a while ago. This person was speaking about the dangers of the occult. He warned his audience that the occultists were making great inroads into our culture—even into the evangelical community. Much of their success, he contended, is due to our lack of vigilance. As an example, he cited the uncritical way in which most Christians read C. S. Lewis's books. Lewis was much too soft on the occult, he said. As an example, he cited the fact that Merlin the Magician is a hero in Lewis's novel *That Hideous Strength*.

The speaker was picking on one of my favorite novels. What he considered to be a defect in Lewis's story, I think of as a strength.

C. S. Lewis was very interested in the relationship of Christianity to magic and fantasy. Like his friend J. R. R. Tolkien, he liked to characterize the Gospel as "the true fairy tale." All the key elements of the fairy story are present in the gospel: the seemingly irreversible bad turn of events (an evil spell, a curse, the presence of a wicked stepparent), the surprising rescue (the princess kisses the frog, Prince Charming finds Sleeping Beauty), and the "happy ever after" ending.

This is not to say that the gospel story is a collection of "cunningly devised myths" (2 Peter 1:16). This is the one fairy story that deals with events that have really happened in history.

Lewis's point is that the gospel is not *less* than an ordinary fairy tale, it is *more*.

Similarly, the gospel isn't less than magic, it is *better* than magic. But what makes it better is that it transforms and fulfills the world of magic. This is what Lewis has in mind when he refers to "the Deeper Magic."[9] The Christian Gospel provides us with all that is legitimate in the ways of the magicians — and more.

Being Like Children

The developmental psychologist Jean Piaget noted that children go through an "animistic" stage in their understanding of physical reality. Ask a little child why trees grow leaves and the child will give an answer that attributes conscious purposes to trees: for example, they grow leaves "because they want to look pretty."

That is the only kind of explanation young children are capable of grasping. The only cause-and-effect relationships they can imagine are those in which the causes are highly "personal" ones. In their view of the world, nature is personified; even the trees have wants and desires.

Occultism often functions as an attempt to retreat into that sort of innocent animism, in which the forests are alive with personalized forces and the stars decide our destinies.

For Christians, this will not do. We have no business trying to escape into the child's naive conception of physical reality. We cannot forget what we know about photosynthesis, nor can we turn the clock back to the days when alchemy and astrology did not have to contend with the findings of biochemistry and astronomy.

The Bible does not ask us to give up our adult ways of viewing reality. Indeed, it explicitly encourages us to grow up. It is good for us to put away the things of our childhood.

I live in a highly populated universe. It has many more conscious beings in it than my secular friends are willing to concede:

God, the archangels, the cherubim and seraphim, Satan and his deputies.

But I don't think of myself as having settled for a simpler, "pre-scientific" view of reality. I don't want less than a scientific naturalism has to offer—I want more. My belief in the reality of God and the angels and the demons isn't grounded in a stubborn refusal to study the world with scientific precision; it is based on the reflective conviction that scientific precision does not give me all the information I need in order to operate with a healthy grasp of reality.

Jesus said, "Truly, I say to you, whoever does not receive the kingdom of God like a child shall not enter it" (Luke 18:17). The Savior was not, however, putting his stamp of approval on infantile regression. There is an important difference between being child*ish* and being child*like*. It is the latter that the gospel encourages.

To be childlike in the Christian sense is to be open to the delights and surprises that come when we are able to look at reality with the eyes of faith. It is to see the universe as a friendly place, not because we have set aside our critical abilities, but because we have formed the very adult conviction that when we uncover the lawlike regularities and cause-and-effect relationships of the world in which we live, we are discovering signs of the faithfulness of the One who is at every moment "upholding the universe by his word of power" (Heb. 1:3).

In the final analysis, the fundamental question is not whether it is legitimate to view the world in highly personalized terms. For Christians that issue rests on something that is even more basic. The only adequate way of personalizing the universe is to come to know the right Person. The gospel presents us with a Savior who is greater than the magicians and shamans, greater than the witches and the warlocks. The only proper way to "reenchant" the universe is to open our lives to the power of Jesus.

The occultists' deep desire to feel at home in a personalized world is a legitimate one. This yearning fits the purposes for which we were all created. But we cannot turn the world into a friendlier place merely by practicing the crafts of the occult "sciences." Indeed, we cannot create a friendlier environment by any craft at all.

Only God can bring the magic back into our lives in a way that allows us to be whole persons in a friendly universe. And God has done this—by the "Deeper Magic" of the cross.

Jesus has died for our sins. And he has been raised from the dead so that we can experience a new power in our lives. The curse has been lifted. We can live happily ever after in his eternal kingdom. We can know "the mystery hidden for ages and generations but now made manifest to the saints . . . which is Christ in you, the hope of glory" (Col. 1:26–27).

"Christ in you, the hope of glory." The one true Ascended Master, who has graced our lives by drawing near to us in order to become our only reliable Spirit Guide!

No occultist could ask for more.

7. Getting Beyond Nothing

A student once told me that he thought I was a nihilist. I had lectured on that subject in class that day, and he said that I presented the case for nihilism with a passion that could only come from someone who was convinced by that viewpoint.

I told him he was wrong. And he told me he was only kidding. But actually he was only partly wrong. And I suspect he was also only half kidding.

This is not an announcement that I really have been a closet nihilist all along. But I must admit that I have been tempted by nihilism. It is my favorite non-Christian worldview. Ever since I began studying philosophy, I have been especially intrigued by the writings of those thinkers whose views border on nihilism— Nietzsche, Camus, Sartre, de Beauvoir.

The Importance of What We Reject

Most of us have favorite errors—at least, those of us who have struggled with questions about the nature of reality. There are folks, of course, who have never thought much about anything; they don't have any favorite errors, because they don't even have any favorite truths. But most of us can name a perspective that we find especially intriguing even though we think it is wrong.

What we believe is very important. But what we don't believe is also important. Often the viewpoints that we explicitly reject have a lot to do with the manner in which we adhere to what we do believe.

I've often thought that it would be a fascinating exercise to ask various Christian leaders what their favorite form of unbelief is. I wonder what the Pope would say. Or Billy Graham. Or Mother Teresa. Or Bishop Tutu.

Anyhow, for what it is worth, mine is nihilism. I certainly prefer it to the non-Christian perspectives I have discussed in previous chapters. I've never been tempted to put my basic trust in scientific reasoning. And although if I work at it I can generate some empathy for the monists and the occultists, their viewpoints really aren't serious options for me. But nihilism is another matter.

I would not insist, of course, that all Christians should choose nihilism as their favorite error. This sort of preference is a good example of what philosophers call a "person-relative" factor. There is no one "correct" favorite error. The perspectives that we view as intriguing but wrong will have much to do with our own personal pilgrimages—and, yes, even with individual tastes. Often this kind of thing hangs on something as simple as the question of who we most enjoy arguing with. I know Christians who look forward to having a Jehovah's Witness knock on the door. Not me—I run for cover. But if perchance an itinerant nihilist were to pass my way, I would be inclined to gear up for a good argument.

"The Last 'Ism'"

Nihil means "nothing." A nihilist is a person who makes an "ism" out of the idea of nothing. Nihilism is a philosophy of radical denial. But a denial of what?

Nihilists deny that anything makes intrinsic sense. Their world is one that is devoid of any built-in meaning and purpose. There are no standards of truth or beauty or goodness. Just nothing.

Helmut Thielicke has aptly characterized nihilism as "the last 'ism.'" Thoroughgoing nihilism is an attitude of ultimate despair. It is a philosophy for the disillusioned. Nihilism is the final posture of those who are convinced that they have been wounded by everything they've tried.

In offering my list of philosophers whom I associate with nihilist tendencies, I described them as having views that *border* on nihilism. None of them is really a thoroughgoing nihilist. Indeed, each of the thinkers I mentioned—Nietzsche, Camus, Sartre, de Beauvoir—found it necessary at one time or another explicitly to deny that he or she was a nihilist. These thinkers are best thought of as near-nihilists.

Indeed, it is not likely that a real nihilist would spend a lot of time arguing the case for nihilism. As Thielicke puts it, thoroughgoing nihilism doesn't really function as a philosophical program that needs to be defended. Genuine nihilism serves no pragmatically chosen goals: "it is content to draw the line and call it quits."[1]

Once a person has really arrived at a nihilistic position—thereby calling it quits—it would seem that there isn't much point in doing anything anymore. Why spend a lot of time trying to convince everyone else that nothing matters?

But we must be careful here. It is futile to think that we can pull off cheap victories over the nihilists with easy refutations. I have learned from experience that it isn't easy to nail a nihilist with a quick argument.

I once knew a professing nihilist; I'll call him Sherman. We taught on the same university campus for a while.

One evening Sherman and I attended a dinner for a visiting scholar. The visitor was Jewish. We were all surprised, then, when Sherman began to tell a series of anti-Semitic jokes. Halfway through that awkward dinner session, Sherman got up and left. The next evening I learned where it was that Sherman had gone. The local newspaper carried a report of a speech he had given to a campus group, his topic: "The Dangers of Anti-Semitism"!

I sought Sherman out to tell him how offended I had been by his dinner-table conversation. I also told him how strange it seemed that he would go off and give a speech criticizing anti-Semitism right after he had told those horrible anti-Semitic stories.

Sherman responded by rehearsing the basics of his nihilistic perspective. There are no objective values, he said. It doesn't matter what we say about anything. Nor do we have any obligation to be consistent. That is precisely why he was anti-Semitic for one half of an evening and anti-anti-Semitic for the other half – to show that he was no slave to consistency or to any other value.

We got into quite a heated argument. Why did he have to "show" anything? I asked Sherman. Wasn't he in his own way a slave to consistency? He *had* to show us that he didn't accept any values. And then he *had* to go off and contradict himself. All just so that no one would ever guess that he consistently held to any position. Isn't that a case of having to work pretty hard at being a good nihilist?

In a sense I was right, he retorted. Certainly there was no need – no obligation – for him to act the way he did. There is no good reason to "show" one's nihilism. But there is no good reason *not* to show it either. The reason he acted the way he did was that he *chose* to act the way he did. Nothing more needed to be said. Indeed, not even that "needed" to be said.

This exchange didn't help me like Sherman any better, but it cured me of any hope I had of coming up with an easy refutation of nihilism. This is why I said earlier that it is *unlikely* that a nihilist would want to spend a lot of time trying to convince others that nihilism is the best viewpoint to adopt. It is unlikely – but it is not unthinkable. There is no good reason to do it. But there isn't any good reason *not* to do it either. Given their understanding of reality, nihilists can do whatever they want.

The Nihilist as Creator

Given the tenor of nihilism, it seems likely that there have been very intelligent nihilists who have never bothered to put their thoughts down on paper. One radical nihilist who did go to the trouble to set forth his views, though, is Max Stirner.

Stirner was a German thinker who was born in 1806 and died in 1856. He is not one of the better known philosophers. I had never heard of him until recently, when I happened upon R. W. K. Paterson's fascinating study *The Nihilistic Egoist: Max Stirner.*

The English title of Stirner's major work is *The Ego and His Own*. This book may well be, Paterson tells us, "the most uncompromising of atheistic manifestoes."[2] Stirner didn't simply deny God's existence; he set out to destroy the very idea of a divine Being. His intention is to eradicate all traces of the eternal Creator from his thinking, so that all that remains is a human self that, as Paterson puts it, "perpetually re-creates from the nothingness to which it is perpetually consigned."[3]

This brief characterization by Paterson refers to three important themes in Stirner's nihilistic portrayal of reality. And even though we can't follow through on all the nuances of his thought here, it will be instructive to take a brief look at each of these themes, since they appear regularly in the writings of nihilists and near-nihilists.

Nothingness. There are philosophers who have written hundreds of pages about "nothingness." That's the sort of thing that leads non-philosophers to poke fun at philosophers. Indeed, sometimes those philosophers who write about nothingness are laughed at even by other philosophers.

Obviously, if you think that nothingness is a topic you can spend a long time discussing, then nothingness has some sort of positive fascination for you. Writing hundreds of pages about nothingness isn't the same as writing hundreds of pages about nothing!

I'm not going to offer an elaborate defense of philosophizing about nothingness. But I do want to point out that at least some of these thinkers who are interested in nothingness are drawing upon a strong biblical motif.

The opening verses of Genesis picture God as calling the world into being out of that which "was without form and void" (Gen. 1:1-2). Christian theologians have traditionally described this bringing forth of earthly reality as an act of creation *ex nihilo*—"out of nothing."

This *ex nihilo* teaching has been a topic of considerable theological discussion, much of it quite technical. And that is a good thing. Important ideas need to be given careful technical attention.

Those of us who like that kind of abstract investigation, though, need to be brought back regularly to the biblical materials that serve as the authoritative reference-point for our theorizings. That is especially important with respect to the creation *ex nihilo* doctrine. The Bible doesn't refer explicitly to the *nihilo*, the nothingness. It uses more graphic images: a "void," a formlessness, a "darkness [that] was upon the face of the deep," the untamed waters.

Here is the picture: the divine Spirit broods over the chaos, in all its dark and formless depths. Then suddenly God speaks, issuing a "Let there be!" And then where there had previously been only the deep and untamed chaos, there was now created reality.

The nihilists and near-nihilists have often been enamored of that picture of God calling forth order and purpose out of the chaotic. The Genesis 1 scenario certainly seemed to be very much on Max Stirner's mind. Let's go back to Paterson's characterization of his nihilism that we quoted earlier: the human self "perpetually re-creates from the nothingness to which it is perpetually consigned." Stirner is borrowing from the biblical account here. To be a nihilist is to face the nothingness. But the nothingness that he has in mind is the original chaos that God encounters in the biblical account.

In a perverse sort of way, Stirner was a strong believer in creation *ex nihilo.* We might say that his view of reality is the same as that laid out in the opening verses of Genesis, except that there is one important factor missing in Stirner's version of the creation story: there is no God.

Friedrich Nietzsche had a very similar view. He told the story of a madman who went around proclaiming that God is dead. The madman image was a poignant one for Nietzsche. He was very disturbed that many of his contemporaries acted as if they could stop believing in God and still leave everything else the way it was. That won't do, Nietzsche insisted. Casual atheism is as confused, in his view of things, as casual Christianity.

To let go of a belief in God, for Nietzsche, was to experience madness. When the divine will disappears from the universe, we are brought back to the primal chaos, the nothingness, the darkness that covers the face of the deep.

Creation. To experience this kind of nothingness is to go back, as it were, to the way things were before God brought forth order out of the chaos. It is to encounter a formlessness that gives no hint of the possibility of that ordered whole that we call the cosmos. The face of the deep knows absolutely nothing yet of goodness and beauty and truth.

Now, what would it take to fill that void with meaning and purpose? The Bible gives a clear answer to this question: only a divine "Let there be" can really produce enough meaning and purpose to fill the void. Only the will of a sovereign God can transform chaos into cosmos.

Again, on this point Stirner and his near-nihilist comrades are quite orthodox. They argue that it takes a God to produce a meaningful, purposeful world in which there are patterns of value that are woven into the very fabric of reality. And since there is no God, we must recognize that we are staring into the chaos.

But we need not simply stay there. If there is no divine Creator to do the job, then we can take the task of creating upon ourselves. To be sure, this is an awesome responsibility—being a creator is not something that comes easily.

It is important to make it clear here that the nihilists and near-nihilists do not claim that we can create the stuff of reality as such. They aren't suggesting that we can utter a word that will make a firmament appear, and then utter another word that will bring forth millions of sea creatures. That's not the kind of creating they are talking about.

They are interested in the creation of meaning and purpose. They see us as creators of the values that we attribute to things. The world of firmaments and sea creatures and birds and trees may *be there*, in some sense. But nothing will really make any sense until we give it sense.

The French existentialist philosopher Simone de Beauvoir was very interested in this act of creating value and meaning. She saw it as a momentous event in which we aren't just defining the world "out there," we are actually creating human nature. This is how she described it:

Dostoevski asserted, "If God does not exist, everything is permitted." Today's believers use this formula for their own advantage. To reestablish man at the heart of his destiny is, they claim, to repudiate all ethics. However, far from God's absence authorizing all license, the contrary is the case, because man is abandoned on the earth, because his acts are definitive, absolute engagements. He bears the responsibility for a world which is not the work of a strange power, but of himself, where his defeats are inscribed, and his victories as well. . . . One cannot start by saying that our earthly destiny *has* or *has not* importance, for it depends upon us to give it importance. It is up to man to make it important to be a man, and he alone can feel his success or failure.[4]

Our efforts to call forth order out of the chaos are "definitive, absolute engagements," just like God's might have been – if there were a God.

Finitude. But none of us is God. The nihilists and near-nihilists are aware of that fact. Indeed, it is a very important theme in their view of reality.

Our acts of creation may be God-like, in that they are "definitive, absolute engagements." But they don't "take" as well as God's act of creation would. That's because there is one big difference between us and the divine Creator: God is eternal and we are not.

When the divine Creator says "Let there be," things really do "be." God's creation sticks.

We are finite, and our creations are grounded in our finitude. They don't "be" as well as the kind of thing a God might produce. And that is a very unpleasant fact to have to live with.

Simone de Beauvoir gives a strong hint of how unpleasant this fact feels to her. We are "abandoned on the earth," she says. She feels God's absence acutely.

To be sure, she would not recommend that we sit around lamenting the fact that there is no God. That would be to refuse to accept the responsibility that God's absence thrusts upon us. But neither should we pretend that a universe without God is a pleasant state of affairs. To live in the light of the facts of the case is both to feel the abandonment and to get on with the business of being a finite creator.

This is where Max Stirner is more of a thoroughgoing nihilist than the existentialist writers—Nietzsche and Sartre and de Beauvoir. As I said earlier, Stirner thought it important to destroy the very idea of a divine Being. As long as we keep thinking about how a God might create, he argued, we will be tempted to set standards that are too high for us to attain. We finite beings can't come up with the kind of product that a God can make. We don't have the resources for that kind of creating.

Actually, Stirner thinks, it's difficult enough for beings like us to hold our own selves together. If there is no God, then nothing really holds together very well, including our own inner lives. If, as the nihilists claim, everything around you is a senseless flux, then you too must be a senseless flux.

This is the way Stirner views reality. Let's recall Paterson's summary of his outlook: the self "perpetually re-creates from the nothingness to which it is perpetually consigned." Note the emphasis on "perpetually." Since what we produce doesn't "be" very well, we have to keep reproducing it at each moment. And this also holds for the self that does the producing. Each of us, too, is a perpetually vanishing "nothing." It takes work to make ourselves "be." And even if we manage to keep ourselves going for a while, what we manage to come up with won't last forever.

Some Obvious Questions

When I talk about this subject in my classroom, it's hard to keep my students calm. By this point in the discussion, hands are waving all over the place. They want to record their objections. And there are some obvious ones to record. Let's give the hand-wavers their opportunity here.

Aren't the nihilists saying that their view is the true one? And if so, what right do they have to claim that, if there are no objec-

tive standards? This is a point of real vulnerability for people who deny any sort of objective criteria for deciding issues of truth and goodness and meaning. When we read Nietzsche or de Beauvoir, for example, they certainly seem to be insisting that they are setting forth views that are worthy of our acceptance. It is perfectly reasonable to ask them in turn: Where did you get these standards of "worthiness" by which you are judging the acceptability of perspectives on reality?

Stirner was aware of this objection—more so than the near-nihilists. In simple terms, his response is this: he is painting a picture in his philosophizing. He's not saying it is a *true* picture—that would be more than he has a right to say. Indeed, the only picture a nihilist has any business painting is one that displays a perspective in which truthfulness is not a thing to be honored. If that sounds paradoxical or self-contradictory, Stirner would say, then so be it.

But isn't there still a conviction at work here that one must live in accordance with one's view of reality? That certainly seems to be the case. This seems especially obvious in the passage I quoted from Simone de Beauvoir. Because there is no God, she says, we bear "responsibility" for our world. Reality "depends upon us to give it importance." Not only are our engagements with the world "definitive" and "absolute," but we seem to have an obligation to *see* them as definitive and absolute. De Beauvoir wants us to be aware of our "success or failure."

Suppose, though, that someone told Simone de Beauvoir that he did not feel like thinking about successes and failures. Nor did he particularly want to worry a lot about accepting responsibility for definitive and absolute engagements with reality. After all, if there is no God, who is going to call us to account for not having lived in accordance with an obligation to invest the world with importance. And where would such an obligation come from anyway?

This is, I think, pretty much what Max Stirner would say to Simone de Beauvoir. He would insist that she is still being controlled by the idea of God. Since God does everything with great seriousness, we must too. But we are free to reject all that, Stirner would say.

Isn't there a notion of obligation or virtue, though, that is still lurking beneath the surface here—even in Stirner? I think so. It is hard to read Simone de Beauvoir's writings without sensing that she really does believe that there is a right way to live—or, perhaps better, a right way to *be*. Both she and Sartre, for example, placed a strong emphasis on avoiding self-deception. We are radically free to create any meaning we choose. And it is important, they insisted, to live in the awareness of this radical freedom. Not to do so was to be caught up in "bad faith."

We have every right to ask de Beauvoir and Sartre, though, what is so bad about "bad faith." Why is it so important to live in the awareness of the way things really are? Suppose, for example, that I were an atheistic existentialist who had an opportunity to take a drug that would produce within me a deep and lifelong conviction that there is a God who created me to promote his glory. Why would it be wrong for me to take this drug? I'm sure the near-nihilists would encourage me not to. And that is because they seem to have a deep commitment to cultivating such traits as courage, honesty, and consistency. But I don't really know how they can defend the "ought-ness" of these virtues in a meaningless universe.

Stirner, though, seems to be a different case. He would say, I think, that I can do anything I want—take drugs, join the Unification Church, become an ardent Cubs fan, commit suicide. Nothing matters. Anything goes.

He would say *that—but would he* mean *it?* I doubt that he could really mean it. I don't believe him when he says, for example, that his philosophizing is only painting pictures—that he doesn't mean to say that his depiction of a nihilistic universe is a true account of the ways things are. I don't believe that he is really only playing around. He is trying to convince us of something; he wants us to accept his view of reality because he believes it is more adequate than the one we are operating with.

That is my Christian attempt to "psych him out." But obviously he would deny the legitimacy of what I have argued. He would say that I am painting a picture too—just as he is. And I don't know what I could say to demonstrate that my way of reading the situation is better than his. All I could do is to hold up the gospel for his consideration, in the hope that its promises might touch those deep spiritual yearnings that are still at work, I believe, in every nihilist's soul.

The American Brand of Nihilism

One of Allan Bloom's major contentions in his best-selling jeremiad *The Closing of the American Mind* is that North American culture has come to be dominated by nihilism. To be sure, it is a peculiarly American brand of nihilism. "It is," says Bloom, "a nihilism with a happy ending."[5]

North Americans have a hard time living with despair, Bloom argues, so we put the best face that we can on the nothingness by wedding our nihilistic beliefs to optimistic self-help therapies. This American nihilism manifests itself as "a mood of moodiness, a vague disquiet. It is nihilism without the abyss."[6] But this doesn't mean it is any less nihilistic. A proper understanding of our widespread "value relativism," Bloom insists, will take us "into very dark regions of the soul."[7]

Our North American nihilism may be homegrown, but the seeds are imported. They are, Bloom insists, German seeds—he is convinced that contemporary nihilism has its origins in Nietzsche's thought. Here's how Bloom defends his analysis: "My insistence on the Germanness of all this is intended not as a know-nothing response to foreign influence, the search for a German intellectual under every bed, but to heighten awareness of where we must look if we are to understand what we are saying and thinking."[8]

I'm not completely convinced by Bloom's account. For one thing, I'm not sure that the nihilism is quite as widespread as he insists it is. He is right, to be sure, in suggesting that we are experiencing a virtual epidemic of "values relativism." But, as we will see in the next chapter, not all relativism is grounded in nihilism.

Nor is it really accurate to blame all nihilism on German philosophy. Bloom is being rather narrow-minded in insisting on "the Germanness of all this." As some critics have pointed out, an equally plausible account of the nihilist lineage can be traced through the British Isles, or we could focus on the development of American pragmatism. And even more ancient antecedents can be established—for example, one can trace a lineage for contemporary nihilism that reaches back to the ancient Sophists.

However, it is even a bit misleading to focus exclusively on formal philosophical influences—not that I think it is wrong to look at philosophical influences. I would be in the wrong business if I felt that way. But the philosophers themselves serve deeper, *spiritual* projects. Stirner and Nietzsche and Sartre and de Beauvoir did not invent the nihilistic perspective; they gave philosophical shape to something that had been around for a long time—ever since the Garden.

Where the Issues Are Joined

I said it earlier: the Evil One is very flexible. He doesn't particularly care which idol we choose to worship, as long as he lures us away from honoring God as God.

But I strongly suspect that Satan has a special affection for the nihilistic version of idolatry. It is the "purest" way of accepting his challenge to "be like God." The nihilistic picture of reality is closest to the way he would like the universe to be.

In nihilism all the pretenses are stripped away. Nihilists know that scientific rationality doesn't give us an adequate picture of what it is all about. They don't nurture optimistic thoughts about merging with the cosmic One, nor do they hold out any hope that the occult crafts will unlock the secrets of reality. Clear-thinking nihilists certainly entertain no American-style illusions that "the face of the deep" is actually one of those smiling

"Happy Faces"! They accept the stark truth that the only alternative to a God-created universe is the chaos.

I like the way that the nihilists set up the alternatives. This is why I said at the beginning of this chapter that nihilism is my favorite non-Christian worldview. Even though they move in exactly the wrong direction, the nihilists and near-nihilists have a very clear sense of what the fundamental issues are.

My own thinking on this subject has been greatly influenced by a wonderful little book, *The Problem of God*, by the Jesuit theologian John Courtney Murray. Father Murray argues that the biblical writers aren't very interested in questions about God's "essence" and "existence." They don't speculate about the deity's metaphysical attributes, nor do they seem to think it important to argue for God's existence. The kind of "problem of God" that is raised in the pages of the Scriptures, says Murray, has to do with God's "presence or transparency and absence or opacity."[9]

The biblical writers ask questions of this sort: Is God here with us right now? What are his intentions? How can we know him? How are we to address him? These questions, Murray observes, "are concrete; they are questions of the moment. They are, in consequence, instant, urgent, and momentous in the full sense. The issues they raise are presented not simply for understanding but for decision."[10]

Murray isn't against asking questions about God's essence and existence, but he wants us to realize that when we wrestle with them we are going beyond the explicit categories of biblical thought. It has often been necessary to do this, since many non-Christian thinkers during the past several centuries have challenged us on the essence and existence issues.

But the nihilists and near-nihilists haven't been very interested in the abstract questions. They have brought "the problem of God" back to the agenda addressed by the biblical writers. As Murray points out, for the nihilists the real question is very simple and concrete: Is God present or absent?[11]

Nihilists and Christians agree that if there is to be meaning and purpose it must be created by volition, by an intelligent will. We agree on what the situation is like prior to creative volition: no form, a void, darkness covering the face of the deep.

The big difference—the *huge* difference—has to do, of course, with what we say next. For the believer, the challenge posed by the chaos is acted upon decisively and irreversibly: "And the Spirit of God was moving over the face of the waters. And God said, 'Let there be . . .'"

For the nihilist, nothing occurs that really eliminates the chaos. Each of us still stares into the face of the deep.

The nihilists know that nothing can match an act of divine creation. A human volition may be the next best thing, but it only deserves to be called "next" and "best" because the best thing doesn't exist. Still, they insist, we have to work with what we have. And since the highest wills in the universe are finite human wills, they will have to serve as our most reliable centers of creativity.

We human beings must brood over the face of the deep. And we must challenge the chaos by issuing our own versions of God's decisive "Let there be . . ."

The differences between Christianity and nihilism on this point are great indeed. Though each places a very strong emphasis on the need to create meaning and purpose *ex nihilo*, they have very different understandings of where that creative source is to be located. For the believer, it can only be found in the Spirit of the living God. For the nihilist, human volition is the only available candidate for creative activity.

The "Nearness" of Nihilism

What a stark contrast! It is difficult to imagine a viewpoint that challenges the Christian view of things more directly. Nihilism is a very explicit distortion of God's truth.

It is that very explicitness, however, that makes it an especially instructive distortion. With other, less blatant, forms of idolatry, we are sometimes inclined to say, "So near, and yet so far." Of nihilism, we can plausibly say, "So far, and yet so near."

Let's take a brief look at some of points where nihilism shows a special "nearness" to biblical thought.

*The importance of the God-notion.*Nihilism is very explicit in encouraging us to think about God. The divine authority theme is, of course, always somewhere present in idolatrous thought. But it is often submerged. Secular humanists, for example, recommend *in effect* that we take over some of God's functions. But they are not always very explicit about this dimension of their position.

The nihilists, however, *are* explicitly concerned with the idea of God. Even Max Stirner, who wants to "destroy" the very idea of God, doesn't really think that this destruction can occur as a once-and-for-all act. Just as we have to keep re-creating ourselves at every point, so also we need to ward off the idea of a deity on a continuing basis.

God is very much on the minds of nihilists and near-nihilists. Awareness of God's nonexistence is, for them, an important part of what it means to be a healthy human being. As Simone de Beauvoir puts it, we need always to be aware of our "abandonment."

Other contemporary varieties of atheism tell us that the very notion of a deity is a part of our primitive past—something we must outgrow. The nihilists, on the other hand, want us to stop believing that there is a God, but they don't want us to stop *thinking* about that Being whom we have thereby eliminated from the universe.

The God-notion is a very crucial element in the "spirituality" of nihilism.

God-like-ness. There is a close connection between the nihilists' insistence on the importance of the God-notion and their understanding of healthy human functioning. If we are going to live in accordance with the way things are, we must deliberately set out to do some of the things that God would have done—if there were a God.

The imitation-of-God theme, then, is central to the nihilist conception of how we ought to put our lives together. In evaluating nihilism from a biblical perspective, it is important to recall our earlier discussion of God-like-ness. In challenging us to "be like God," the Temptor is not foisting a blatant falsehood on us—he is distorting a profound truth. We *are* like God. The question is not *whether* we should imitate the Creator, but *how* we should do so.

The Creation of Values. Allan Bloom captures the nihilists' attitude toward moral decision making when he attributes to them the idea that we are value-creating, not value-discovering, beings. This is a clear way of stating the contrast between the Christian and the nihilist perspectives.

We must not allow this way of putting the difference, however, to obscure a real point of agreement. Both believers and nihilists believe that values are basically created. Like the nihilists, I believe that values are the result of an act of creation, but since God is the value-creator, I must be content to be a value-discoverer.

Values aren't just *there,* as a reality that needs no explanation—contrary to what Bloom and other humanists seem to think. Values are issued. The big disagreement between Christians and nihilists is over who does the basic issuing.

The fact that Christians disagree with nihilists about who the ultimate creator is doesn't mean, though, that we should have no interest in fostering a sense of responsible creativity in our own lives.

Indeed, the idea of an imitative creativity has been a favorite theme of many Christian thinkers. It figures prominently, for example, in Dorothy Sayers's writings about the artistic process.

Nihilists are the most radical defenders of the idea of human autonomy. "Autonomy" means "self-legislating." Immanuel Kant is the philosopher best known for his emphasis on the autonomy of the moral decision maker. Kant insisted that if we are to be truly moral agents we will have to think of ourselves as freely creating the universal prescriptive laws that in turn guide our actions.

The nihilists and near-nihilists don't think Kant was clear enough, though, on the requirements of genuine autonomy.

They point out that Kant still thought that we can only rightly choose those laws that conform to the requirements of universalizing reason, that is, laws that we arrive at by asking, "what if everyone did that?" In that way, they insist, Kant was actually placing important restrictions on what we can legislate. After all, in a universe where God is absent, why do we have to be rational in what we choose? Why couldn't we just decide to be irrational?

The nihilists want to throw off everything that might place limits on what we can choose. And that is very bad. The nihilist way of understanding autonomy is blatantly anti-God. But it is not without its positive lessons. In removing the shackles that other philosophies have imposed upon human decision making, the nihilists are conducting an important investigation of the boundaries of human responsibility.

Dialogue with Nihilists

Nihilism need not be viewed only as anti-God. Its "no!" is not merely directed against religious belief; it is also intended as an angry rejection of those secular philosophers who want to get rid of God but retain the meaning and purpose that pervades God's creation. The nihilists recognize that if there is no God then there can be no inherent meaning in the universe.

There is much to learn from nihilism's trenchant critique of other non-Christian perspectives. And there is much to learn from nihilism's critique of the way we Christians have often set forth our views.

José Miguez Bonino has argued that Christians ought to be eager to consider the criticisms that Marxists lodge against Christian thought and practice, even if those criticisms are grounded in a distorted view of reality. Marxism condemns belief in God as such. But the Bible, Miguez observes, condemns idolatry.[11] It may be, then, that what the Marxist intends as a criticism of belief in God might actually be a legitimate criticism of the way we sometimes worship idols.

The same thing can be said about what we might learn from

nihilism. In wrestling carefully with nihilism's misdirected criticisms of a belief in God, we might actually understand more clearly what it means to live responsibly before the face of God. And we might even gain new opportunities to tell nihilists that the very real challenge of the chaos has been eternally settled.

Dialogue with nihilists is well worth the effort. After all, both parties to the dialogue have *nothing* to lose!

8. Relating to Relativism

It was only a brief story on the nightly news. And since it happened in the 1960s, I recall very few of the details. But I do clearly remember the words one of the students shouted into the reporter's microphone.

The scene was a university campus. A professor had been suspended from his job for some kind of sexual misconduct. He was a popular teacher and the students were upset. Since the incident happened during a decade when student demonstrations occurred at the drop of a hat, a group of students began picketing the administration building, demanding the professor's immediate reinstatement.

The television reporter gave an on-the-scene report. He described the situation, then walked over to the crowd of chanting students. He asked a young woman a question, but a male student pushed in front of her and yelled his message into the mike: "We're dealing with morality here! Morality is a relative matter! You can't impose morality on other people!"

Those three sentences always come to my mind when I think about relativism. Actually, they weren't mere sentences. They were proclamations—and three very distinct ones at that.

I once attended a church for a while where the preacher's sermons always had three points. Every week he would print them in the church bulletin in the form of three sentences. I would read the sentences while sitting in church waiting for the service to start. They never seemed to have much to do with each other; only after the preacher had explained himself at great length could I see how they hung together.

This student's three sentences reminded me of that preacher's three points. They were three theses whose relation to each other are not at all obvious to me. I wish I could have questioned the young man. I would like to find out how he would have filled in the paragraphs needed to connect his three staccato-delivered points.

Let me explain my puzzlement.

"We're dealing with morality here." From the way he put the emphasis on "morality" I thought he was going to make a very different point than his other two sentences went on to suggest.

Remember, this was the 1960s, a time when people were also demonstrating about civil rights and the war in Vietnam.

I participated in some of those demonstrations. We talked a lot about morality. We were fond of saying, "We're dealing with *morality* here." "The Selma police chief says that it's simply a question of law and order. But that *isn't* simply what it's all about. We're dealing with *morality* here!" Or: "President Johnson is wrong. It's not just a matter of defending our interests in Southeast Asia. We're dealing with *morality* here!"

That's how that sentence was often used in the 1960s. So when this young man shouted it into the microphone, I expected him to go on to express some noble moral sentiment—to say something about the right to a fair trial, or about people being innocent-until-proven-guilty, or about the need to give people a second chance. I didn't expect his second sentence at all.

"Morality is a relative matter!" That wasn't the kind of line you heard much in the civil rights and antiwar demonstrations. Try to think about what it would have been like if Martin Luther King, Jr., had defended the cause of racial justice by proclaiming, "Morality is a relative matter!" Imagine war resisters painting that sentence on the signs they used when they picketed the White House.

I wonder if this young man would have used that sentence if he were demonstrating about something other than sex. Maybe he was only meaning to say that *sexual* morality is a relative matter. I wish the reporter had asked him to elaborate.

"You can't impose morality on other people!" This third sentence is even more of a puzzler. The most bothersome word in it

is the "can't." If, for example, "you can't" means "it is physically impossible to," then the student was simply misinformed. The dean of the university *had* imposed his moral convictions on other people. He had successfully suspended the professor for doing something that had offended the moral sensibilities of a group of university administrators.

Or maybe the student meant to say that it wasn't *wise* to do this sort of thing. Perhaps he was convinced that suspending people for sexual practices always or usually backfires. If that is what he was getting at, though, then I wonder why he acted as if what he was saying was so obviously true. University deans get away with all sorts of things that students don't like.

There is yet another possible interpretation of the "can't" in this third sentence. The student might have meant it as an "ought not to." I'm reluctant to push this interpretation, because this is to imply that the student really was very confused. But I can think of no other meaning that captures the prophetic certainty with which he spoke. Here, then, is how I am inclined to interpret his sentence: "One ought not to impose one's moral oughts on others."

Now that is a strange thing for the student to say. It would mean that he was doing the very thing that he was insisting ought not to be done. He was imposing his own "ought" on the dean.

The Challenge of Relativism

It might seem that I've just been toying with the sentences the student uttered. But from my point of view I am paying him a genuine compliment: I don't think that his position is as relativistic as it first appeared to be.

I don't mean to suggest that all relativists are confused, or that no one ever succeeds in the attempt to be a real relativist. It may turn out, of course, that it is impossible to hold to a thoroughgoing relativism in a sincere and consistent manner. But that would have to be demonstrated by careful arguments. And though I have my own hunches on the subject, I don't have an arsenal of conclusive arguments to back them up.

Philosophers have devoted much time to debating the pros and cons of relativism. A serious investigation of the issues at stake requires a patient attention to their fine points of argumentation. There is much to be learned from those technical discussions; I think Christians should take that kind of careful debate very seriously.

But that is not the challenge I mean to take up in this chapter. It's not my aim here to supply Christians with ammunition that will help them to refute the claims of the relativists. I am more interested in promoting the sort of conversation that will enable us Christians to learn from the relativists. I would also like us to be able to respond to the relativists with the kind of credibility that can only come from an honest wrestling with their concerns.

To say this sort of thing is, of course, to run the real risk of sounding wishy-washy. This is a good point in the discussion, then, for me to appeal to the authority of Jerry Falwell.

Reverend Falwell has been no friend of relativism. A few years ago he edited a book that was written by some professors who taught at his Liberty University. It is a well-argued case for a robust conservative Protestantism. Falwell and his colleagues insist that it is important for their kind of fundamentalist Christians to take a strong stand in favor of moral "absolutes." One of their criticisms of the kind of broader evangelicalism that I favor is that we evangelical intellectuals have been too soft on relativism, and we have been too willing to enter into a nonjudgmental "dialogue" with our opponents.

After laying all that out, however, Falwell and his associates turn to a critical examination of their own brand of conservative Protestantism, setting forth some major weaknesses in the fundamentalist movement with which they themselves identify. They don't pull any punches. With remarkable candor they criticize their fellow fundamentalists for such things as being afraid of self-criticism, overemphasizing minor theological points, engaging in hero worship, and so on.

Of special significance for our present discussion is what they have to say about the *way* their kind of Christians have insisted on the importance of moral "absolutes." This point hasn't always been pursued in a healthy manner, Falwell and his colleagues observe. Fundamentalists, they argue, tend to approach

every conceivable issue with a totally black-or-white mentality. Our tendency is to view something as either totally right or totally wrong. While this is definitely the case in many situations, becoming locked into that kind of mentality has caused overstatement and overcriticism in many unnecessary matters.[1]

I agree with what these fundamentalist writers are saying here. Indeed, they seem to be recommending the very sort of flexibility and balanced approach that they have criticized the evangelical intellectuals for advocating.

But since Falwell and his friends have already insisted that we evangelicals are too soft on relativism, they are forced to find a different way of describing their own "softening" position. So they invent a new label: they say that fundamentalist Christians must do a better job of avoiding "overabsolutism."

I'm perfectly willing to go along with this new nomenclature. From here on in, if people accuse me of being soft on relativism, I'm going to tell them that they have misunderstood what I have been saying. All I'm doing, I'll say, is following through on a piece of advice I got from Jerry Falwell. I have joined Jerry Falwell's crusade against "over-absolutism"!

Relativism's Different Moods

I don't, however, share Falwell's skepticism about engaging in dialogue with our non-Christian opponents. I still think it is important to engage in a give-and-take conversation with people who advocate relativism. There are several reasons why I feel strongly about this need. Let me mention two of them here.

The first is a general consideration—one that I have already emphasized at earlier points in this discussion. It has to do with honesty. We must not attribute viewpoints to our opponents that they don't really accept. And this means that we must make sure that we have understood their position. If we Christians really do believe in moral absolutes, then the obligation to tell the truth is surely one of them. It would be a very strange sort of morality indeed that permitted us to bear false witness against our relativist neighbors in order to promote the cause of absolute values!

The second reason is based upon my own experience. I have actually learned much by taking the views of relativists seriously.

One thing I have learned is that there are very different relativistic moods. The student who blurted his three-point sermon outline into the reporter's microphone had a very arrogant tone. He *wanted* to be a relativist, even though, as it turns out, he probably wasn't a very consistent one.

But that is by no means the universal mood among relativist thinkers. Christians are often quite unfair to relativists in this regard. They imagine that every person who claims to be a relativist is bent upon undermining traditional morality. On the contrary, there are relativists who, if they could undermine anything, would undermine their own relativistic morality.

Consider the well-known British philosopher Bertrand Russell. Russell was not a religious believer, by any stretch of the imagination. He even wrote a book with the title *Why I Am Not a Christian*. Throughout his distinguished career he often made it clear that he thought morality had no objective basis. But Russell was not happy about his relativism, a fact that he regularly admitted in his writings.

For example, Russell intensely disliked Nietzsche's perspective on life (even though it is generally agreed among scholars that Russell didn't understand Nietzsche's philosophy very well). He genuinely wished he could find a way of refuting what he took to be this very wicked perspective on things.

Russell once gave very poignant expression to this wish. In a chapter on Nietzsche in one of his books, he imagined what it would be like if Nietzsche and Buddha were called to debate their respective philosophies of life before the judgment seat of the Almighty.

Buddha begins the debate by describing the immense suffering that occurs in the universe. He details the plight of the poor, the diseased, the outcast, and the oppressed. The only thing that can deliver us from this travail, Buddha insists, is a way of salvation that is rooted in universal love.

Nietzsche responds by characterizing Buddha's preachments as "the degenerate fear-ridden maunderings of this wretched psychopath." Why should we "go about snivelling because trivial people suffer?" The misfortunes of the weak are nothing compared to the splendor that we see in the lives of those powerful individuals who were not afraid to achieve greatness by exercising the will-to-power—fierce conquerors, like Alcibiades and Napoleon.

Buddha will have nothing of this. The only kind of power that truly brings greatness, he replies, is the power that manifests itself in "love and knowledge and delight in beauty."

Nietzsche's response is derisive. A world filled with those commodities would be an insipid one. If Buddha's way should win out, Nietzsche complains, "we should all die of boredom."

Having laid out the issues in this imaginative fashion, Russell offers his own assessment of the debate:

> For my part, I agree with Buddha as I have imagined him. But I do not know how to prove that he is right by any argument such as can be used in a mathematical or a scientific question. I dislike Nietzsche because he likes the contemplation of pain, because he erects conceit into a duty, because the men whom he most admires are conquerors, whose glory is cleverness in causing men to die. But I think the ultimate argument against his philosophy, as against any unpleasant but internally self-consistent ethic, lies not in an appeal to facts, but in an appeal to the emotions. Nietzsche despises universal love; I feel it the motive power to all that I desire as regards the world. His followers have had their innings, but we may hope that it is coming rapidly to an end.[2]

These are not the arrogant comments of a person who wants to live in a universe governed by moral relativism. Russell can see no legitimate alternative to relativism, but he clearly wishes that there *were* one. He would like to be able to show that an ethic based on love is the right one to accept and that a might-makes-right perspective is wrong.

Relativism Versus Christianity

Moral relativism is the view that there is no final court of appeal that decides for us that one basic moral perspective is better, or truer, or more adequate, than any other one. Or to put it differently, it is the view that there are as many final courts of appeal as there are moral perspectives. If we really have gotten down to basics in a moral dispute, and if we have arrived at conflicting but sincerely held moral perspectives, then there is no way of adjudicating the argument.

That's the way Russell sees the debate between Buddha and Nietzsche. The conflict is a basic one: Buddha says that the love of others is the highest good, and Nietzsche insists that self-asserting power is the ultimate. And that's where argumentation has to stop, Russell says.

Not that Russell wants it to stop there. Russell doesn't like Nietzsche's viewpoint. He sees no way of refuting Nietzsche, however, by way of "any argument such as can be used in a mathematical or a scientific question." And since Russell is convinced that mathematical proofs and scientific experimentation are the only ways of knowing available to human beings, there is really nothing more that can be said about the merits or demerits of Nietzsche's viewpoint. We still might try to influence Nietzsche's "emotions," in the hope of bringing about some sort of moral conversion, but we have thereby left the realm of rational discourse behind us. Russell and Buddha "feel" positively toward the love of neighbor, while Nietzsche "despises" it. That's the way it stands.

But that's not where a Christian can allow it to stand. The Bible gives us a very different picture. It informs us that people can be very sincere in their moral convictions and still be dead wrong:

"There is a way which seems right to a man, but its end is the way to death" (Prov. 14:12).

From a biblical viewpoint, there *is* a final court of appeals for deciding these issues. Human beings may argue with each other until they seem to reach a stalemate. But after all that is humanly possible has been said and done, there is a still a point of view that needs to be taken into account: *God's* perspective, the point of view of a sovereign Creator who is perfect in wisdom and goodness, and who has chosen to make his moral preferences known to us. In the prophet's striking phrase, God "has shown us what is good" (Mic. 6:8).

Bertrand Russell may have been a relativist, but he had a clear sense of the significance that a belief in God has for this topic. In an essay he once wrote about the influences on his intellectual development, he reflected on the important example set for him by his "Puritan" grandmother:

She wished her children and grandchildren to live useful and virtuous lives, but had no desire that they should achieve what others would regard as success, or that they should marry "well." She had the Protestant belief in private judgment and the supremacy of the individual conscience. On my twelfth birthday she gave me a Bible (which I still possess), and wrote her favorite texts on the fly-leaf. One of them was "Thou shalt not follow a multitude to do evil;" another, "Be strong, and of good courage; be not afraid, neither be Thou dismayed; for the Lord Thy God is with thee whithersoever thou goest." These texts have profoundly influenced my life, and still seemed to retain some meaning after I had ceased to believe in God.[3]

To repeat: Russell was no friend of revealed religion. But when it came to thinking about the vindication of our moral convictions, he clearly longed for access to a God-like perspective on things. And he felt very ill at ease in a universe where no such perspective was available.

It may seem that in his assessment of religious belief Russell wanted to have it both ways. And he as much as said so himself, later on in the same essay in which he talked about his grandmother's influence on his moral outlook: "Those who attempt to make a religion of humanism, which recognizes nothing greater than man," he confessed, "do not satisfy my emotions. . . .And so my intellect goes with the humanists, though my emotions violently rebel. In this respect, the 'consolations of philosophy' are not for me."[4]

"Schools" of Relativism

Relativism isn't the same kind of "ism" as the others we have discussed. Relativism is a more general pattern of thought. Each of the others — humanism, monism, occultism, nihilism — is a more specific "school" of relativism. Let's look at the ways in which each of our four other "isms" appropriate relativistic themes.

Humanism. Of the adherents to these four schools, the secular humanists have been the least explicit about their relativism. Some humanists have boasted of being able to give to values a more solid "scientific" grounding than the older religious perspectives were able to provide. Others have insisted that the business of making moral judgments must now be treated as as an experimental, tentative, trial-and-error activity — much like the testing of empirical hypotheses. Still others have conceded that morality has a strong and unavoidable "subjective" element, but they have argued that scientific reasoning can go a long way in helping to eliminate unnecessary superstition and dogmatism from the patterns of our moral decision making.

Monism. The monists celebrate the fact of moral disagreement. For them, relativism is something to be fretted about only if we insist on restricting ourselves to the "older" consciousness, with its either-or kind of thinking.

In the monist view, ultimate reality is a creative energy that feeds on the interaction between polarities. Since all of our diverse thoughts and inclinations will ultimately be absorbed into the One, there is nothing in our present dichotomies that will be wasted. What some call "good" and what others call "evil" is all a natural part of the process of making new connections and achieving new unities. Both Attila the Hun and Mother Teresa are necessary moments in our journey toward oneness.

Occultism. As we saw in our discussion of the occultism phenomenon, many people are attracted today to occult beliefs and practices because they are looking for moral authority. They want a perspective that transcends the babble of human opinions.

That doesn't mean, though, that devotees of the occult are necessarily searching for moral absolutes. They are on the look-out for moral voices that transcend *human* confusions, but they seem to be quite willing to tolerate a little confusion in the spirit world.

The morality of the occultists seems to be quite similar to that of ancient polytheism. They are willing to tolerate the existence of a multiplicity of "gods," just as long as they get to have their own tribal deity. The people who take Mafu seriously aren't necessarily convinced that Mafu is the greatest and wisest of all ascended masters. The important thing is that he is *their* ascended master.

Occultism transfers relativism into the spirit world itself.

Nihilism. I said earlier that nihilism is my favorite non-Christian philosophical perspective. It is also my favorite form of relativism.

Indeed, one reason I nurture some admiration for Bertrand Russell is that, although he is basically a secular humanist, in moral matters he moves closer to the nihilists. He is convinced that the question of divine authority is important for deciding whether relativism is true or not. If there is a God, then there is a way of deciding which moral perspective is ultimately the correct one. But if there isn't a God, then it's just a matter of "emotions." Since Russell is an unbeliever, he is a relativist. But not a very happy one.

From a Christian point of view, Russell poses the challenge at the right point. Again, Russell's position on this point is essentially the nihilist one. And as Father Murray noted, the nihilists formulate the problem in exactly the same way as the biblical writers. The real issue is God's presence or absence.

Christian Absolutism

If I am forced to choose between absolutism and relativism, I come down clearly on the side of absolutism. To borrow Francis Schaeffer's apt phrase, I believe in "the God who is there." All true morality is grounded in the will of an all-wise and all-good Creator.

But I am somewhat nervous about the "absolutism" label—not because I don't think that there are absolutes, but because I worry a little about what it means to attach an "ism" to my belief in absolutes.

I'm not so nervous, though, that I am ready to the abandon the term altogether. Sometimes it is important to adopt labels even when we are nervous about doing so. And there is at least one good reason for me to call myself an absolutist: it at least communicates the important information that I am not a relativist!

Perhaps my nervousness is adequately dealt with by lining up with Jerry Falwell in his opposition to *over*absolutizing. But then it becomes quite important to be clear about how we understand the more modest absolutism to which we are thereby committing ourselves.

Here are some of the clarifications that I think are necessary.

Christian absolutism doesn't apply to every detail of the moral life. To be an absolutist doesn't mean that I have to be absolutely sure about everything. God has provided us with clear and eternally reliable guidance about the basic issues of life. But that doesn't eliminate all the puzzles and ambiguities.

This isn't primarily an ethics book, so I won't pursue this topic in any detail. But Christians seem to need constant reminders that there are many things that are "person-relative." This is what Jerry Falwell and his colleagues were getting at when they criticized the overabsolutizers for dealing with "every conceivable issue with a totally black-or-white mentality."

Moral decision making isn't always simply a matter of applying absolutes to clear-cut situations. We regularly face contexts in which we cannot avoid allowing personal preferences and "judgment calls" to come into play. Sometimes two Christians will rightly sense very different obligations in a given situation because they are pursuing different callings or they have formed different loyalties along life's way. And there are also those times when the most we can hope for is to get out of a bad situation without making an even worse mess of things.

Christian absolutism doesn't mean that the absolutes are fully known to us. It's one thing to believe that there *are* absolutes. It's quite another thing for people to claim that they have a perfect grasp of what those absolutes are all about. Christians would do well to keep these two things clearly distinguished in their own minds.

There are two distances that separate us from a complete knowledge of the absolutes by which we guide our lives.

The first is the distance between creature and Creator. This is an eternal distance. It will never go away. Since God is infinite and we are finite, we will never know as God knows. This means that there may very well be dimensions of God's moral standards that we will never fully understand.

The second distance separates the way we are now from the way we will someday be. "We shall be changed." We will never know as God knows. But we will someday understand things much better than we do now: "For now we see in a mirror dimly, but then face to face. Now I know in part; then I shall understand fully, even as I have been fully understood" (1 Cor. 13:12).

Christian absolutism doesn't mean that divine absolutes are to be identified with a particular cultural perspective. Earlier we discussed Jesus' work as a unifier. He is putting together a new kind of race and priesthood and nation. To become a follower of Jesus Christ is, we might say, to be given a new "culture"—new values, new ways of feeling and thinking and acting.

Jesus is creating a new community that draws its membership from every tribe and tongue and people of the earth. Jesus doesn't want to make us all into white North Americans—or into Swedes or Zulus or Koreans or Brazilians. He wants us to receive the new identity that comes from being incorporated into the kingdom of God. And that kingdom is very much a cross-cultural phenomenon.

In *The Closing of the American Mind*, Allan Bloom is very critical of the requirement that university students take courses in non-Western cultures. He sees this requirement as being motivated by "a demagogic intention." Educators want "to force students to recognize that there are other ways of thinking and that Western ways are not better." What these teachers fail to tell us, though, is that all these non-Western cultural perspectives "think their way is the best way, and all others are inferior."[5]

The contemporary emphasis on cross-cultural studies is, Bloom insists, self-defeating. Students are exposed to cultures that have no appreciation for scientific ways of solving problems. So the students are encouraged to empathize with people who denigrate science. But the stated reason for this exposure is to get the students to see the dangers of ethnocentrism. And since the scientific outlook is the only true antidote to ethnocentrism, the result is confusion:

This is what really follows from the study of non-Western cultures proposed for undergraduates. It points them back to passionate attachment to their own and away from the science which liberates them from it. Science now appears as a threat to culture and a dangerous uprooting charm. In short, they are lost in a no-man's-land between the goodness of knowing and the goodness of culture, where they have been placed by their teachers who no longer have the resources to guide them. Help must be sought elsewhere.[6]

Bloom is right to be concerned about ethnocentrism. And he is probably also correct in suggesting that cross-cultural studies are often conducted in a confused manner. But his own prescriptions do not succeed in providing the necessary correctives.

I'm not antiscience, but I don't agree with Bloom's insistence that it is science alone that truly "liberates us" from ethnocentrism. Science is no liberator. It cannot provide us with the resources that will save us from our narrow-mindedness and mean-spiritedness. Hitler employed some brilliant scientists who were nonetheless committed to a very vicious kind of ethno-centrism!

Those contemporary movements, such as monism and occultism, that are critical of scientific rationality are surely confused in many ways. But the people who are attracted to these movements are motivated, I am convinced, by a legitimate dissatisfaction with a worldview that glorifies scientific rationality as a "liberator."

Science itself needs to be "tamed." It needs to find its proper place in the larger human quest. And that can only happen if we can see the big picture, so that we will know how to assign science its rightful role in our explorations of the nature of reality.

That same big picture can help us to evaluate the contributions of diverse cultures, including our own. Only when we have that larger perspective on things can we begin to fit together the pieces of the cross-cultural puzzle.

The word of God provides us with that larger perspective. Biblical religion is a strong opponent of ethnocentrism. People who confuse Christian absolutes with the values of their own particular culture haven't really grasped the big picture.

Christian absolutism doesn't ignore our subjective lives. There has been a revival of "virtue ethics" among Christian ethicists in recent years. For a long time there was an undue emphasis on the morality of actions, rules, and goals—with little attention to our subjective dispositions. Christian thinkers have been correcting this.

My own thinking has been influenced by these discussions of Christian virtue. That influence showed up in earlier chapters, when I emphasized the importance of being *truthful* Christians.

Many people tend to think of inviolable rules and regulations when they hear about "absolutes." Don't steal. Don't commit adultery. Don't cuss.

These prescriptions are, however, only the tip of the moral iceberg. There is an inner "depth" that God also requires of us. It's not enough to refrain from stealing; we must cultivate a subjective respect for others persons and their property. It isn't sufficient that we not sleep around or that we keep ourselves from uttering naughty words; it is also important to be faithful and gentle people.

I've already referred to the prophet Micah's proclamation that the Lord has *shown* us what to do. That's a good text for illustrating that God has provided us with firm moral guidance, but it's also interesting to see how Micah fills in the moral details: "and what does the Lord require of you but to do justice, and to love kindness, and to walk humbly with your God?" (Mic. 6:8).

Unfortunately, experience teaches us that justice, kindness, and humility aren't necessarily the moral traits that we can expect to find in the people who talk the most about the need for "absolutes."

Living with Complications

There are Christian scholars who are convinced that relativism is, in the final analysis, an incoherent perspective. They argue that you can't even say that relativism is true — or that it is "better" than absolutism — without thereby undermining the very case you want to defend.

They may be right. Even if they were to lay out their argument in a very convincing manner, however, they still would not have dealt a death blow to relativism. For one thing, there may be people who aren't all that embarrassed about being shown to be incoherent. We saw that syndrome at work in Max Stirner and his picture-painting view of philosophy: he was a nihilist who was not at all concerned about whether his relativism could be formulated in a coherent manner.

Furthermore, even if we could convince people that there are absolutes, we have not thereby brought them to obedience to the divine will. The Christian version of absolutism won't always be the one that is most attractive to people who are inclined to accept absolutes.

It isn't easy to be a Christian absolutist. The decision to devote one's life to serving God and neighbor doesn't automatically lead to neatly packaged solutions to the basic issues of human living. Indeed, being a Christian often complicates matters.

The most important "absolute" that biblical religion presents us with is an absolutely reliable Person. The laws and rules and principles that are given to us for our guidance are not the ultimate reference point in our lives. They are the instruments by which our divine Guide directs us on our journey.

This strong emphasis on personal guidance was already present in the Old Testament. God issued his commandments to the people of Israel. But he knew that this was not enough to give them adequate direction as they made their way through the wilderness. So he provided them with more: "Behold, I send an angel before you, to guard you on the way and to bring you to the place which I have prepared" Exod. 23:20).

In the New Testament we are provided with a form of divine guidance that is even more personal. God took all of our struggles upon himself in an intimate way; he became flesh and dwelt among us. That doesn't mean that all the moral struggles have gone away. But it does mean that we can approach them in the quiet confidence expressed by the black slave spiritual: "Nobody knows the trouble I've seen, nobody knows but Jesus."

We have been given a wonderful gift that we can in turn offer to the relativists: a Guide who knows the trouble we've seen, and who is leading us in the right direction.

The moral trouble doesn't magically disappear from the Christian life. But we are given the assurance that our present struggles and confusions will eventually be cleared up—when we arrive at "the place which I have prepared."

9. Integrated Journeying

The anthropologist James Peacock tells the story of a Russian factory worker who regularly pushed a wheelbarrow home from work. Since the wheelbarrow was always empty, the guards at the factory's security checkpoint always allowed him to proceed through the gate with nothing more than a quick glance and a nod of the head. It was only after many months went by that the authorities discovered that the man had been stealing wheelbarrows!

Peacock uses that story to emphasize the importance of looking at the larger context. We fail to see important dimensions of reality, he says, when we follow our common tendency "to inspect the contents and not the container, to focus, too narrowly, on the parts and not the whole."[1]

Peacock's advice applies equally well to Christian attempts to understand non-Christian "isms." We often don't pay close enough attention to the wheelbarrows. We are more inclined to zero in on the specific contents. Some new "ism" comes along, and we inspect it by itemizing its teachings: what does it say about the existence of a personal God? the Trinity? biblical authority? heaven and hell? and so on, down the list.

To be sure, the "isms" I have featured in this book fail that kind of test miserably. And let it be said: it is bad to fail that test.

Secular humanism denies the possibility of revealed knowledge. That is very bad.

Monism tries to do away with the Creator-creature distinction. That is very bad.

Occultism encourages people to flirt with demonic powers. That is very bad.

Nihilism views the human will as the source of all authority in the universe. That is very bad.

Relativism claims that one set of values is as good as any other. That is very bad.

We can establish that each of these perspectives gets a failing grade, though, yet still miss out on what is going on with these viewpoints in the larger sense. How does each of these non-Christian perspectives hang together as an attractive way of viewing reality? What are the legitimate spiritual yearnings that these "isms" are addressing? What are the cultural forces that give rise to these ways of looking at the world?

These are the questions I have been trying to pay attention to in this book. I have attempted to keep an eye on the larger context—the wheelbarrows.

Looking at Our Own Wheelbarrows

It is time now, though, for me to say something about the need to inspect our own wheelbarrows. In doing so I am offering my final line of defense for the approach I have been recommending in the previous chapters. I have been insisting that it is a good thing for Christians to put the best face they can on non-Christian "isms." And I have argued that we can fulfill this assignment only if we take the larger contexts seriously.

I can imagine some Christians feeling a bit nervous about my approach. They will worry that I have been too charitable—that I have not been harsh enough on occultism, for example. I don't know what more to say by way of putting their minds and hearts at ease without talking about how I would like my *own* perspective on life to be treated.

Ultimately my defense of the need to focus on the larger context in evaluating non-Christian "isms" is an appeal to the Golden Rule. In assessing people's basic perspectives on reality, I want us to do unto to others in the way that we would have them do unto us.

We Christians ought to welcome it when other people take a

careful look at our own basic hopes and fears—and not just to show that we are willing to be vulnerable enough to have others probe beneath the surface of our specific beliefs. To ask others to inspect our spiritual yearnings is a way of inviting them to take a very serious look at the Christian way of understanding reality.

This contention is worthy of a little elaboration.

Hopes and fears are driving forces in the human spirit. Earlier I argued that we humans are basically trusting beings. Trustings, I said, are the steering mechanisms that drive us along on our journeys.

I don't mean to contradict that point by characterizing hopes and fears as our basic driving forces. To struggle with the question of trust is to wrestle with hopes and fears.

These categories—trust, hope, fear—are very significant for evaluating religious belief. Without paying attention to these matters, for example, it is very difficult to know what is going on in many seemingly abstract theological discussions.

I once heard an unbeliever ask a Christian philosopher this question: "Why do you make so much of the idea of a Supreme Being, a deity who manifests all of these perfections—perfect goodness, perfect power, perfect knowledge? Why do you *care* so much whether that kind of God exists?"

The philosopher gave a memorable response. "Let's put it in very simple terms," he said. "I care whether there is a God who is a supremely perfect Being because I need a very *big* God. And that's because only a very *big* God can deal with a very big problem that I have. We Christians call that problem sin. When I go to church and pray that old prayer, 'We have strayed from thy ways like lost sheep, and there is no health in us, have mercy upon us, most merciful God,'—when I say those words I am confessing a problem I have that is very real. And it runs very deep."

The philosopher continued: "To deal with my problem of guilt and inadequacy requires a mercy that is bigger than I can manufacture myself. If it's going to work, it's even got to be bigger than anything the whole human race working together can manufacture. Only an infinite mercy—a *supreme* love and grace—can solve my deeply felt problem. That's why I care so much whether a supremely perfect divine Being exists. My problem of sin is so big that only an infinitely big God could solve it."

That is a helpful way of putting it. And it is a way that focuses on hopes and fears. It shows the unbeliever how the seemingly abstract elements of Christian theology have to be understood as responses to yearnings that arise out of the depths of our humanness.

But hopes and fears are only a part of the picture. Christian belief isn't simply a matter of finding beliefs that match up well with our hopes and fears. If it were, then the Freudians would be right when they argue that religion is only "wish-fulfillment."

That's not to say that we have to be eager to refute all charges of wish-fulfillment. It is crucial to our understanding of the way things are that God has fashioned us in such a way that there will be a close fit between what we wish were true and what really is true. That's the point of Saint Augustine's famous prayer: we have been created in such a way that our hearts will be restless until they rest in God.

But it isn't simply a business of believing whatever fulfills our wishes. Though the affective dimension of our lives is very important to our Christian quest, it also needs to be disciplined by the cognitive. We cannot avoid careful reflection on the reasonableness of the ways in which we look for wish-fulfillment. The Bible itself underscores the necessity of this: "Always be prepared to make a defense to any one who calls you to account for the hope that is in you, yet do it with gentleness and reverence" (1 Pet. 3:15).

Integrating our Lives

A mindless wish-fulfillment approach to religion isn't healthy. But neither is an approach that encourages rational reflection to remain aloof from an awareness of our deepest human hopes and fears.

How do we hold it all together in a workable fashion? To ask this is to point to the need for integration.

Integration, like *integrity*, is a word that is used to express the value of wholeness. To work for integration is to attempt to get the parts together in such a way that they form a healthier whole. A person who has integrity is someone in whom we can see how the pieces all fit together.

How can we achieve more integrated lives? I have no "secrets for integrated living" to offer, but I can provide a few general suggestions for clarifying the subject.

Integration requires selecting among potentials. One of my favorite books about Christian feminism is *All We're Meant to Be*, by Nancy Hardesty and Letha Scanzoni. Their title nicely captures the way the Bible portrays the quest for human potential. We human beings have to be what we are *meant* to be.

That may not be the same as what we *want* to be, of course. When we start thinking in terms of what we are meant to be we are raising the question of the purposes of human life. And I don't know of any better brief account of those purposes than the famous lines of the Westminster Shorter Catechism: that our "chief end" as human beings "is to glorify God and enjoy him forever."

We human beings were created to serve God's purposes. And God in turn loves us and wants us to be healthy, well-functioning individuals.

There are many people who would find it offensive to be told that their purpose for being is to please the God who made them. They want to "be their own person," without having any external demands or restrictions placed on them.

It's this "I've got to be me" spirit that has often been at work in the present-day emphasis on realizing human potentials. But when we think about it carefully, it turns out to be quite difficult to maximize our potentials without having any sort of pattern to guide us.

The record shows that I have never been an outstanding athlete. Even if I had worked at it very hard, I would never have been one of the better athletes around. But there is no doubt in my mind that I could become a much better athlete than I am right now. Suppose, for example, that I decided to spend four hours a day doing nothing but practicing foul shots on the basketball court. Or what if I set up my teaching schedule so that I could spend every morning at the bowling alley? It's not too late for me to make significant progress in these activities.

I have other untapped potentials. I once had twelve years of violin lessons, but it has been a long time since I have held that instrument in my hands. Suppose I were to take it up again? Or suppose I were to devote myself to the serious study of sculpture?

I choose these examples precisely because they have to do with activities in which I am not a promising candidate for stardom. My point is, though, that I could be better than I am if I set myself to the task—even though my "better" would be someone else's mediocre!

And if my goal in life were to "realize my potentials," or to be more "well-rounded as a person," I might be well advised to work hard at bowling and violin playing and sculpturing. But none of us has the time to realize potentials in an unqualified way. Even if I were to take on the assignments I just mentioned, I would still have been rather selective. Why bowling rather than tennis? Why the violin rather than the tuba? Why sculpture rather than watercolors?

This is why I like the emphasis on "all we are *meant* to be." Trying to be all that we *can* be is an impossible assignment. Out of the vast array of human potentials, we must find out what it is *good* for us to be. For the Christian, this means that we must consult the will of our Creator.

Integration requires a pattern. To integrate our lives, we need a pattern to guide us.

This pattern will include some very general guidance about what goes into a well-constructed human life as such. For one thing, the Bible makes it clear that certain kinds of moderation and balance are good for all of us. To live a well-formed life is to place some limits on, for example, the satisfying of our physical and economic hungers.

But not everyone will integrate the diverse elements of their lives in exactly the same way. What it means for one of Mother Teresa's co-workers in Calcutta to integrate her life will differ significantly from the way it is done by a Chicago real estate agent who is also a wife and a mother and a church elder.

Many of us also have to think about "corrective" adjustments. If I am a very emotional kind of person, I may have to work a little harder than others at making sure that rational reflection plays a role in my life. Or the other way around.

Integration is a complicated business. It takes into account an overall picture of what we think we are meant to be. Even the people who claim to be realizing their "full potential" are actually being guided by some notion of what kind of person they think they ought to be.

For Christians, the pattern is grounded in God's revelation regarding his purposes for us. But there is more to finding that pattern than simply reading the Bible or listening to sermons. We have to pray for guidance and talk to friends and visit counselors and read biographies of people who have lived faithful Christian lives—among other things.

Integration is a process. Full integration is a goal that we aim at. We shouldn't expect ourselves simply to *be* integrated. Our lives are processes that are moving toward an integration that we have not yet attained. This is why the idea of a human life as a journey is such a helpful one.

The journeying, or pilgrimage, image has long been a favorite of Christians, but it has recently been given considerable attention by non-Christians.

In the past, Christians have often used the pilgrimage notion to reinforce an unhealthy pattern of "otherworldliness." We have viewed our present lives as a journey that we are taking through a foreign country. Since our final destination is heaven, we have reasoned, we really don't belong in this world. Therefore, we don't have to worry too much about trying to correct the injustice and poverty and oppression that we see along the way.

This has been an unfortunate application of the journeying motif. But that doesn't mean we should do away with the pilgrimage idea entirely. It can also be a healthy theme. It can give us a sense that our lives have unity, without requiring us simply to *be* unified beings. We are not yet unified beings—but we are moving toward that goal. The unity we experience is the kind of unity a story has. Our lives have a unified plot—we are in the middle of our narrative. The happy ending has not yet occurred.

The New Age movement has been aware of the strengths of this journeying theme. We noticed earlier that the New Agers have been very critical of the kind of narcissistic "atomism" that sees people as isolated centers of pleasure seeking. The monists are looking for "connectedness."

The "I do my thing, you do your thing" narcissism of Fritz Perls not only saw us as disconnected from each other; it also portrayed our inner lives as a series of disconnected states. The narcissistic atomists viewed healthy living as going from one disconnected subjective state of feeling to another: "I used to be threatened by that kind of thing; now I'm pretty comfortable with it." There is no recognizable plot in this flow of consciousness.

One very good thing about New Age monism is its insistence that this kind of inner disconnectedness is not healthy. The monists see their lives as journeys, or pilgrimages. Journeys are not just aimless wanderings; they are mapped out. The New Agers have recognized that it is important for us as pilgrims to know where we have been and where we are going. We might even think of the space-age journey of "RiLeschardlie" as a pagan updating of John Bunyan's *Pilgrim's Progress*.

Contemporary monists are interested in integrated living. And they know that integration is a process that occurs on a journey. We can be grateful that they have reminded us of this fact.

Pilgrim Witnessing

These considerations about integration are important to keep in mind as we Christians attempt to become more whole persons. They are also important themes to remember as we witness to non-Christians about our faith.

We want others to know that we are trying to become more integrated people, and that we have discovered an exciting, biblically grounded pattern for attaining this goal. Even though we are not yet whole persons, we are on the journey that the Apostle Paul described: he hadn't yet reached the goal of perfection, he said, "but I press on to make it my own, because Christ Jesus has made me his own" (Phil. 3:12).

We want other people to recognize our pilgrim status. But this means that we must also take *their* pilgrimages into account.

In the preceding chapters I have been offering, in effect, a pilgrimage analysis of some prominent non-Christian "isms." In doing so, I have tried to avoid the rather mechanical checklist approach that Christians often use to show that Christianity has a superior set of beliefs.

I hope that I have offered sufficient evidence that I do take the truth value of a person's beliefs very seriously. Indeed, this conviction about the importance of the belief content of our lives is crucial to the account of integrated living that I have been offering in this chapter.

The cognitive part of our lives—the part of us that engages in rational evaluation of beliefs, to see whether or not they are plausible accounts of reality—is one very important dimension of humanness. In saying this I mean to emphasize two things. First, cognition *is* important. And second, it is only *one* of the important things. Both of these statements are necessary to my evaluation of non-Christian "isms."

As a philosopher I am extremely interested in what people believe. But I also want to know *why* they believe what they do. The "why" question includes a focus on the evidence or grounds for what a person believes. When I read about the folks who listen to Penny Torres as she "channels" Mafu, I want to know what reason they have for thinking that they are actually listening to the authoritative voice of a legitimate spiritual "master." And, frankly, I don't think the rational basis for that belief comes to much.

But my interest in the "why" of the belief in Mafu doesn't end there. I also want to know why these folks find that belief so attractive. What hopes and fears does it speak to? And why have they become so disillusioned with their earlier beliefs—whether they were the tenets of secular humanism or Christianity or Judaism—that they have now become enthusiastic participants in channeling sessions?

Pilgrimage Analysis

When I stress the importance of pilgrimage analysis, I don't mean to insist that every person we speak to is on a discernible journey. Some people really are aimless wanderers. They drift from one disconnected situation to another. One reason why Fritz Perls's atomistic narcissism was so popular for a while is that his account of the flow of consciousness actually fit the experience of many disconnected people.

But it is important at least to look for evidences of a journey in a person's life. Indeed, this can be an important service we can perform for others—to help them clarify their own itinerary.

Pilgrimage analysis—attempting to understand people's itinerary—will attend to at least three factors.

First, pilgrimage analysis looks for the hopes and fears that fuel a person's journey. The story is told that when the writer Gertrude Stein was on her deathbed, a friend asked her, in an anguished tone of voice, "Gertrude, Gertrude, what is the answer?" Ms. Stein quietly responded: "What is the question?"

That story has the feel of an apocryphal tale, but I like it anyway. It is important to know what questions people are asking before we provide them with answers. This is especially true of the "big" questions about life.

I once spent an evening with an old friend. I hadn't seen him for a number of years, and I had heard that since we had last been together he had rejected Christianity. Not too long after we had renewed our acquaintance, I started to quiz him about his spiritual attitudes and beliefs. Actually, I peppered him with questions about sin and salvation and God and eternity.

He got very angry with me, and after a while he refused to continue the conversation. Several weeks later I received a long letter from him. He told me about the deep pain he had felt in his relationship with his strict Christian parents. Then he outlined the difficulties he had been experiencing in holding his marriage together. He talked about having flunked out of a graduate program. Then he told me about the number of times he had been close to suicide in recent months.

He had been looking forward to visiting with me, he said. He had thought of me as someone who would accept him as he was, and also as someone who would be there when he was ready again, someday, to talk about the "big" issues of sin and salvation, God and eternity. Right now, though, he was not prepared to argue about those questions. "This month, I'm just trying to stay alive."

His letter made me very angry with myself. What he had needed was someone to offer him gentle encouragement, someone to hear the story of his pilgrimage. Instead, I had come on like a dogmatic inquisitor, challenging him to provide clear answers to abstract theological questions.

My questions were not bad ones. They dealt with very important issues. But they were not the questions he was prepared to address at that stage in his journey. He was operating on a much more elemental level, asking whether there was any human being who could simply reach out to him as a friend in the midst of his confusion and desperation.

That episode is, for me, an especially poignant reminder of the need to engage in an analysis of the actual hopes and fears of the people to whom we wish to speak about issues of eternal importance.

Second, pilgrimage analysis looks at the options that a person has rejected. This concern has already surfaced many times in this book. I have repeatedly insisted that it is important to know what people are reacting against. If we view occultism, for example, simply as a rejection of the gospel, we will fail to grasp what is going on in the hearts and minds of many people who embrace this perspective. Contemporary occultists are often in a severe reaction against a thoroughgoing secular humanism. They are eager to reenchant a world that has become devoid of mystery and magic.

When we attempt to understand the disillusionments of our neighbors, we have a better idea of how to introduce them to the riches of the Christian message.

Third, pilgrimage analysis attempts to look at the direction in which a person is moving. I often wonder what it would have been like if some of my evangelical friends had had an opportunity to talk with C. S. Lewis during the year or so prior to his conversion to Christianity.

At one point during that period, for example, Lewis believed in an abstract divine Being of sorts, but not the Christian God. As Lewis tells his story in *Surprised by Joy,* he had become convinced that it was necessary to affirm the existence of a divine Absolute, but this was not a God with whom one could have a personal relationship—certainly not a God who would choose to become incarnate in Jesus Christ.

Suppose I, as a strict conservative Protestant, had had the opportunity to quiz Lewis during this period. And suppose, having heard his account of the nature of the deity, I had responded in this manner: "Your theology is wholly inadequate. The divine Absolute you describe cannot save you from your sins. This God of yours seems to be more of an abstract construct than a living Redeemer to whom one can pray. If that's all the theology you can come up with, you're in big trouble!"

These are, in a sense, legitimate comments about Lewis's religious outlook at that point in his life, but they fail to take into account the larger picture of what was happening to him.

Within a year, Lewis would be a Christian. And when he looked back on this earlier perspective from that vantage point, he saw it as a significant move in the direction of Christianity. Far more important than the specific cognitive content of his rather vague notion of a deity was the fact that he was gradually yielding his heart and mind to the living God.

Here's how Lewis described what he was going through during this period:

> Perhaps, even now, my Absolute Spirit still differed in some way from the God of religion. The real issue was not, or not yet, there. The real terror was that if you seriously believed in even such a "God" or "Spirit" as I admitted, a wholly new situation developed. As the dry bones shook and came together in that dreadful valley of Ezekiel's, so now a philosophical theorem, cerebrally entertained, began to stir and heave and throw off its gravecloths, and stood upright and became a living presence. I was to be allowed to play at philosophy no longer. It might, as I say, still be true that my "Spirit" differed in some way from "the God of popular religion." My Adversary waived the point. It sank into utter unimportance. He would not argue about it. He only said, "I am the Lord"; "I am that I am"; "I am."[2]

It is one thing to evaluate a set a beliefs strictly on the grounds of their theological and philosophical merits. It is another thing to see how those beliefs fit into the larger context of a person's spiritual pilgrimage.

Apostolic Awkwardness

I'm a religiously awkward person. I make a lot of foolish mistakes in my spiritual life. I try out theological ideas that later strike me as so strange that I wonder how I could have given them even a moment's thought. I study books about prayer and contemplation, and then when I try out the techniques that they prescribe, I feel quite silly. I'm glad God has a sense of humor. And I'm glad he decided to equip me with one, too!

That's not to say that all of my spiritual mistakes are due to simple awkwardness. Many of my problems stem from sheer perversity on my part. But awkwardness is also prominent in my spiritual life.

I suspect I'm not unique in this regard. Indeed, I tend to work on that assumption when I evaluate the words and deeds of other Christians. I assume that many of their mistakes are due to the kind of awkwardness I perceive in myself.

Because of this I tend to be impatient with Christians who don't admit to any awkwardness in their own attempts to please God, and who refuse, in their evaluations of other Christians, to grant any role to awkwardness.

There are some Christian writers, for example, who seem to think that the best way of highlighting the threats posed by a perspective like monism or occultism is by warning that these "isms" are making inroads into the Christian community. They warn against Christian teachers who, as they view things, have been enlisted—wittingly or unwittingly—into serving the cause of "the aquarian conspiracy." Or they bemoan a Christian "drift toward paganism." Or they accuse their fellow Christians of dabbling in "shamanism."

There are two things that I find disturbing about these accusatory accounts. One is the apparent assumption that things would be just fine in the Christian community if only people would stop exploring commonalities with non-Christian perspectives. I reject that assumption. I think we Christians will have a healthy faith only if we continue to wrestle seriously with the challenges posed by various "isms" that come along. When I see my neighbors turning to these beliefs, I want to know what makes them so attractive and how we Christians can better speak to their hopes and fears.

The other disturbing thing is the insensitivity that these writers show to the role that awkwardness plays in our Christian lives.

The last chapter of Revelation provides us with a marvellous example of apostolic awkwardness. What makes this example especially striking is that it appears in a very solemn setting.

As the biblical record draws to a close, the Apostle John has just been provided with a glorious vision of the New Jerusalem. In Revelation 21, an angel was sent to him with this invitation: "Come, I will show you the Bride, the wife of the Lamb" (v. 9). John is carried to a high mountain where he sees the Holy City in all its splendor. There follows an almost breathless account of the magnificent scene that is spread out before him.

Then in the final chapter of Revelation, John recounts this little episode:

> I John am he who heard and saw these things. And when I heard and saw them, I fell down to worship at the feet of the angel who showed them to me; but he said to me, "You must not do that! I am a fellow servant with you and your brethren the prophets, and with those who keep the words of this book. Worship God."
>
> (Rev. 22:8–9)

This is a marvelous example of apostolic awkwardness. The apostle has just been granted a privileged glimpse into the glorious future God is preparing. John is so overwhelmed by what he has experienced that he becomes momentarily disoriented. Sensing the need to respond in gratitude, he falls down to worship the angel who has been his guide during this final vision.

Suppose that we came upon this scene without knowing anything about the context. It would be shocking to see an apostle trying to worship an angel! Worshiping a creature rather than the Creator is an act of idolatry, and idolatry is what sinful rebellion against God is all about.

But John is not condemned as an idolator. He receives nothing more than a mild reprimand. Indeed, it is hardly even a reprimand. The angelic response to John's action is more like a gentle reminder. The angel knows that the apostle is momentarily disoriented. The tone of his remarks suggests this meaning: "Quick, get up! You're not supposed to bow down to angels. Only *God* deserves to be worshiped."

I'm glad this little episode is included in the Bible. It makes me more comfortable with my own regular bouts of spiritual disorientation. This brief account lets me know that God expects us to be a bit awkward at times in our religious behavior.

And if not even the apostles were exempt from such displays of human frailty, we should not be too harsh with contemporary Christian leaders when they show occasional signs of spiritual awkwardness. We can be patient with them when they get briefly sidetracked by a strange idea, or when they experiment with techniques that turn out to be misconceived, or when they choose the wrong words to express what they are trying to say.

That doesn't mean that we should not be on guard against deceptive doctrines and perverse practices. The Book of Revelation is itself full of warnings against such threats. But it also concludes with this delightful example of a well-meaning apostle who experiences temporary spiritual confusion. Revelation contains many warnings against false teachers, but it also contains a warning, here in this concluding episode, against being too harsh with momentarily confused apostles. We mustn't be too quick to assume that everyone who bows down before an angel is a wicked idolator!

Like the Apostle John, we contemporary Christians are people who have been given glimpses of the divine glory. And like him, we are often very awkward in our responses to what the Lord has shown us.

But we should not let ourselves off too easily. We are also regularly plagued by the spirit of rebellion that caught hold of our first parents in the Garden. The echoes of the serpent's taunting challenge still ring in our ears. We are tempted to be our own gods. We want to run the whole show by ourselves.

But those are minor themes in the overall plot of the stories we are living out.

We have also heard the good news. And we have embarked on a new and exciting pilgrimage.

We are on our way to becoming more fully human.

We are discovering new unities in the universe.

The magic has come back into our lives.

The threat of nothingness is disappearing.

We are learning how to live with the fact that we don't know everything.

And we have been given the assurance that our very real hopes and fears are "met" in the One who walks with us on our journey.

Notes

Chapter 1

1. Don Richardson, *Peace Child* (Glendale, CA: Regal Books, 1974)
2. Kosuke Koyama, *Waterbuffalo Theology* (Maryknoll, NY: Orbis Books), p. 91.
3. George E. Reedy, *The Twilight of the Presidency*, 1st ed. (New York: New American Library, 1970), pp. 183–184.

Chapter 2

1. Tim La Haye, *The Battle for the Mind* (Old Tappan, NJ: Flemming H. Revell, 1980).
2. Abraham Kuyper, *Lectures on Calvinsim* (Grand Rapids, MI: William B. Eerdmans Publishing, 1931), pp. 130–34.
3. John Calvin, *Institutes of the Christian Religion*, trans. Ford Lewis Battles (Philadelphia: Westminster Press, 1960), bk. 4, chap. 10, sec. 12.

Chapter 3

1. Jeffrey Burton Russell, "Deep Magic Never Dies," *Commonweal*, March 25, 1988, p. 187.
2. Sissela Bok, *Lying: Moral Choice in Public and Private Life* (New York: Random House, 1978).
3. Augustine, *Of True Religion* (Chicago: Henry Regnery Co., 1959), pp. 64–66.

Chapter 4

1. "Humanist Manifesto II," reprinted in Paul Kurtz, *In Defense of Secular Humanism* (Buffalo, NY: Prometheus Books, 1983), p. 41.
2. Ibid., p. 118.
3. Ibid.
4. Ibid.

Chapter 5

1. Richard Bach, *One: A Novel* (New York: William Morrow, 1988), p. 12.
2. Ibid., p. 174.
3. Fritjof Capra, *The Tao of Physics* (Berkeley, CA: Shambhala, 1975), p. 11.
4. Christopher Lasch, *The Culture of Narcissism: American Life in an Age of Diminishing Expectations* (New York: Warner Books, 1979), p. 21.
5. Frederick S. Perls, *Gestalt Therapy Verbatim*, ed. John O. Stevens (New York: Bantam Books, 1969), p. 4.
6. Henry F. May, *The Enlightenment in America* (New York: Oxford University Press, 1976), p. xiv.

7. G. K. Chesterton, *Orthodoxy* (Garden City, NY: Doubleday, 1959), p. 131.

8. Ibid., p. 132.

9. Georgios I. Mantzaridis, *The Deification of Man* (New York: St. Vladimir's Seminary Press, 1984), pp. 42, 122.

10. C. S. Lewis, *The Weight of Glory and Other Addresses* (London: Macmillan, 1949), pp. 13–15.

Chapter 6

1. B. F. Skinner, *Beyond Freedom and Dignity* (New York: Alfred A. Knopf, 1971), p. 7.

2. Robert Galbreath, "Explaining Modern Occultism," in *The Occult in America: New Historical Perspectives*, ed. Howard Kerr and Charles L. Crow (Chicago: University of Illinois Press, 1983), p. 20.

3. Max Weber, "Science as Vocation," in *From Max Weber: Essays in Sociology*, trans. H. H. Gerth and C. Wright Mills (New York: Oxford University Press, 1946), p. 139.

4. Peter L. Berger, *Facing Up to Modernity: Excursions in Society, Politics, and Religion* (New York: Basic Books, 1977), pp. 209–210.

5. Douglas R. Groothuis, *Unmasking the New Age* (Downers Grove, IL: InterVarsity Press, 1986), p. 159.

6. Bruno Bettleheim, *The Uses of Enchantment: The Meaning and Importance of Fairy Tales* (New York: Vintage Books, 1977), p. 45.

7. Ibid., p. 51.

8. Helmut Thielicke, *Nihilism: Its Origin and Nature—with a Christian Answer*, trans. John W. Doberstein (New York: Harper & Row, 1961), p. 81.

9. C. S. Lewis, *The Lion, the Witch and the Wardrobe* (New York: Macmillan Publishing, 1950), pp. 159–60.

Chapter 7

1. Thielicke, *Nihilism*, p. 29.

2. R. W. K. Paterson, *The Nihilistic Egoist: Max Stirner* (New York: Oxford University Press, 1971), p. 192.

3. Ibid., p. 217.

4. Simone de Beauvoir, *The Ethics of Ambiguity*, trans. Bernard Prechtman (New York: Citadel Press, 1964), p. 17.

5. Allan Bloom, *The Closing of the American Mind: How Higher Education Has Failed Democracy and Impoverished the Souls of Today's Students* (New York: Simon & Schuster, 1987), p. 147.

6. Ibid., p. 155.

7. Ibid., p. 151.

8. Ibid., p. 152.

9. John Courtney Murray, S.J., *The Problem of God: Yesterday and Today* (New Haven: Yale University Press, 1964), p. 119.

10. Ibid., p. 23.

11. Ibid., p. 210.

12. José Míguez Bonino, *Christians and Marxists: The Mutual Challenge to Revolution* (Grand Rapids, MI: William B. Eerdmans Publishing, 1976), p. 70.

Chapter 8

1. *The Fundamentalist Phenomenon: The Resurgence of Conservative Christianity,* ed. Jerry Falwell, with Ed Dobson and Ed Hindson (Garden City, NY: Doubleday, 1981), p. 183.
2. Bertrand Russell, *A History of Western Philosophy: And Its Connection with Political and Social Circumstances from the Earliest Times to the Present Day* (New York: Simon & Schuster, 1945), pp. 772-773.
3. Bertrand Russell, "My Mental Development," in *The Philosophy of Bertrand Russell,* ed. Paul Arthur Schilpp (New York: Harper & Row, 1963), vol. 1, p. 5.
4. Ibid., pp. 19-20.
5. Bloom, *Closing of the American Mind,* p. 36.
6. Ibid., p. 37.

Chapter 9

1. James L. Peacock, *The Anthropological Lens: Harsh Light, Soft Focus* (New York: Cambridge University Press, 1986), p. 11.
2. C. S. Lewis, *Surprised by Joy: The Shape of My Early Life* (New York: Harcourt Brace Jovanovich, 1955), p. 227.